Course	Introduction to Philosophy
Course Number	**PHIL 100**
Professor	Jeff Vanderpool
	PHIL 100 Fullerton College

http://create.mheducation.com

ISBN-10: 1308137818   ISBN-13: 9781308137810

Contents

Credits

CHAPTER **10**

*O*ur Knowledge
of the World around Us

As the poet said, "Only God can make a tree"—probably because it's so hard to figure out how to get the bark on.

—WOODY ALLEN,
ON SEEING A TREE IN SUMMER (2007)

10.1. Vats and Demons

A human brain has inputs and outputs. The inputs are signals from the person's eyes and ears and other sense organs. The brain receives those inputs and processes the information. The outputs are signals that the brain sends to various parts of the body. Those signals may cause us to breath, blink, laugh, walk up a flight of stairs, and so on.

Now imagine that we have better technology. Suppose that, in our advanced world, a scientist removes someone's brain and keeps it alive in a vat of nutrients. The scientist hooks up this brain to a computer that supplies it with the kind of inputs that normally come from the eyes and ears. If the computer does its job well enough, then the person won't be able to tell the difference. His brain will process the inputs in the same way it once processed inputs from the eyes and ears. His brain will then produce outputs, which are transmitted back to the computer. The computer will return new inputs, and the saga will continue.

In this scenario, the person whose brain is in the vat will have normal experiences. From his point of view, nothing special is happening. He will meet his friends, go to work, have dinner, and watch TV. Or, at least, he will believe he is doing those things. In fact, his life will be a computer-generated illusion.

125

Now suppose it is suggested that you are that person—you are a brain in a vat, and your "life" is only an illusion. You may think you are reading a chapter in a book right now, but in fact the computer is only creating the illusion that you are. This suggestion seems absurd, but how could you prove it wrong? You can do nothing, it seems, to prove that your life is real. After all, every experience you have, including the experience of trying to prove you're not a brain in a vat, could be supplied by the computer. You might protest that the whole story is technologically impossible—brains cannot be kept alive in vats, nor can computers sustain such illusions. But perhaps that is true only in your artificial, deluded world. In the real world, outside your vat, such computers do exist.

The Matrix (1999), a movie starring Keanu Reeves, explores this possibility. In the movie, people's brains are not removed, but their bodies are connected to a giant computer that achieves the same effect. The people in the Matrix believe that they live in a physical world of buildings and weather and cars, but in fact that world exists only in their minds. *The Thirteenth Floor* (1999) and *Total Recall* (1990) exploit similar themes.

Long before there were movies and computers, René Descartes (1596–1650) dreamed up a similar scenario. Rather than imagining brains in vats, Descartes imagined that a powerful "evil spirit" was intent upon deceiving him—a spirit with godlike powers that wanted to fool him about everything. This spirit can not only manipulate Descartes' experiences, but it can also manipulate his beliefs. If such an Evil Demon tried to deceive *you*, what would happen? Presumably, you would acquire false beliefs about everything. You would think that $3 + 3 = 5$, and that belief would seem as certain to you as $3 + 2 = 5$ now does. You might be sure about everything, yet right about nothing. And how could you possibly figure out what was really going on? Every thought you might have could be manipulated by the Demon.

Descartes also wondered how we can know we're not dreaming. Often, we have vivid dreams in which we believe absurd things. Perhaps, right now, you are dreaming, and the thoughts you're having are absurd, but you're too confused to realize this. According to Descartes, "there are no conclusive indications by which waking life can be distinguished from sleep." *Inception* (2010), a Christopher Nolan film, utilizes this theme. In that movie, characters are constantly trying to figure out whether they're in a dream (or in a dream within a dream!), and doing so is not always easy.

The problem is not merely to say how we can *know for sure* that there's no Demon, that we're not dreaming, and that we're not brains in vats; the problem is how we can offer any evidence at all against these possibilities. Any alleged evidence we produce might just as easily be produced by a brain in a vat; and any confidence we have on these matters might have been planted in us by the Evil Demon, or might be due to our confusion inside a dream.

We'll return to these ideas later. But first, let's consider another outrageous possibility, which some philosophers believe describes the real world.

10.2. Idealism

When you look at a tree, what exactly do you see? One answer is that you see a patchwork of colors, mainly shades of brown and green. If you move your head, the pattern shifts slightly. Close your eyes, and the pattern disappears. The tree is still there, of course, but the thing you were experiencing—the splash of colors—will vanish. Open your eyes, and it will reappear.

The seventeenth-century philosophers called this pattern of colors an *idea* in your mind. In the twentieth century, the term *sense-datum* was popular. Today, philosophers speak of *qualia*. But whatever term is used, the point is that what you literally see is not the tree itself. What you literally see is a representation in your mind. This representation changes when you look at the tree from different angles. But the tree, presumably, remains the same. A color-blind person might have a different experience when looking at the tree. Rather than green and brown, she might see shades of purple.

But now a startling possibility arises. If we experience only ideas, then why do we need "physical objects" as part of our worldview? What do they add? We are never aware of them. Of course, we might say that physical objects are the *cause* of our ideas: we experience a patchwork of brown and green colors because there is a tree out there, causing us to have these experiences. But that hypothesis can never be proved. We can never step outside of our ideas to find their cause: no matter how we look at the tree (or touch it, or smell it), we will encounter only more ideas. The physical world is thus an unnecessary supposition, so we might as well forget about it. *The only things that really exist are our minds and their ideas.*

This conclusion was embraced by George Berkeley (pronounced BARK-lee), an eccentric but brilliant Irish bishop who lived from 1685 to 1753. His writings have a vigor and incisiveness that have earned them a permanent place in intellectual history. The theory that reality consists entirely of minds and their ideas is called "Berkelian Idealism" in his honor—if it is an honor. Berkeley's summation of this view is admirably clear:

> though it were possible that solid, figured, movable substances may exist without the mind . . . yet how [could we] know this? Either we must know it by sense or by reason. As for our senses, by them we have the knowledge only of our sensations, ideas, or those things that are immediately perceived by sense, call them what you will; but they do not inform us that things exist without the mind, or unperceived. . . . It remains therefore that if we have any knowledge at all of external things, it must be by reason, inferring their existence from what is immediately perceived by sense. But what reason can induce us to believe the existence of [physical objects], from what we perceive, since the very patrons of matter themselves do not pretend there is any necessary connection [between physical objects] and our ideas?

Idealism strikes most of us as absurd because it denies that physical objects exist. But aside from insulting the view, what can we say against it? A number of objections come to mind. When I look at the tree outside my window, why do I always experience the same splash of colors? You and I can say, "Because you're always looking at the same tree." What can an idealist say? He doesn't believe there is a tree. Or, when you and I both look out my window, why do we both see the same kind of thing? Again, we can say it's because we're seeing the same tree; but the idealist must call it a coincidence. And again: When I start the dishwasher and later come back to unload it, it appears as though something has been going on in my absence—the dishes have been getting cleaned. But what can Berkeley say? On his view there is no dishwasher, and there are no dishes. These objections to Idealism all boil down to the same thing: It seems that there is a world independent of us—a world that affects the same person similarly at different times, that affects different people similarly, and that keeps going when we're not perceiving it.

Bishop Berkeley responded to these objections by bringing in God. God is responsible for ordering our ideas so that we can make sense of the world. When we are both looking through the same window, God makes sure we have the same experiences. And when I come back to unload the dishes, God makes sure that the dishes look clean. In fact, God saw them being cleaned—even when no one is looking at the tree or the dishes, they still exist as ideas in God's mind. God is always perceiving everything.

If, in response, the "materialist" challenges Berkeley to prove that God exists, Berkeley might offer some of the traditional arguments for God's existence. Or he might say, "To make sense of my theory, I have proposed that we accept the existence of one thing in addition to minds and ideas—namely, God. However, believers in an independent, physical reality are proposing that we accept the existence of countless additional things—namely, every single physical object in the universe. My hypothesis is simpler."

10.3. What Evidence for These Views Might Be Like

So far, we've been discussing ideas that almost no one believes are true. There are no idealists, despite Berkeley's arguments. And, aside from a few lunatics, nobody believes they're a brain in a vat or that an Evil Demon controls their thoughts. However, views like these could turn out to be true.

Suppose that, when you finish reading this paragraph, there is a sudden discontinuity in your experience. In an eye blink, you find that you are in a hospital bed. Across the room is a mirror, and in the mirror you see an unfamiliar person with bandages on his (or her) head. You are feeling confused and panicky, when a doctor comes in and explains what is going on. She says that your brain was just removed from a vat, where it had been connected to a computer for many years, and reinstalled in your head. You are given a tour of the facility, where you see other brains connected by wires to the colossal computer. Then, leaving the hospital, you find that you are in a city that you have never heard of and that your "hometown" does not exist on any map. If you had those experiences, it would be reasonable for you to conclude that you had been a brain in a vat.

Or instead, suppose that, after you finish reading this paragraph, the world begins to tremble and everything around you dissolves—all the buildings, trees, and even the ground melts away, leaving nothing but a white-tinged background. Other than being confused, you feel no discomfort. Then it is all replaced by a different, strange-looking environment, which in turn disappears, to be replaced by still another environment. After this happens a few times, you hear a booming voice, coming from everywhere at once. The voice identifies itself as God, and it explains that He has been giving you a demonstration of His powers. There are no "physical objects," He explains; they are unnecessary—why should He create physical objects to cause you to have experiences when He can give you the experiences directly? If all this happened, it would be reasonable for you to believe in Idealism. And if the booming voice had instead described a battle in which He had triumphed over the Evil Demon, then, given enough detail, it could be reasonable for you to accept the existence of Descartes' evil deceiver.

If any of these things happened, you would not be forced to change your worldview. Instead, you could conclude that you had gone crazy. But it would at least be clear that you possessed evidence for Idealism, or for the Evil Demon, or for the brain-in-a-vat hypothesis. Of course, as things stand, we have no such evidence. However, we have not yet offered any reason to *reject* these crazy ideas, either. Can we come up with any?

10.4. Descartes' Theological Response

Descartes was the first person to consider this question. He lived in the early seventeenth century, when modern science was very young. Descartes was excited about the development of science, and he wondered whether scientific knowledge had secure foundations. In fact, Descartes wondered if *any* of our beliefs were on firm footing, since science is just the rigorous application of common sense to the study of the world.

For our knowledge to be secure, Descartes thought, it must ultimately rest on foundations that cannot be doubted.

Thus, Descartes hoped to find an absolutely certain ground for human knowledge. And he thought he did, in the following chain of reasoning:

(1) What can I know for sure? If I seem to see a fireplace in front of me, or even if I believe that 2 + 3 = 5, I can't be sure of these things because an evil spirit might be controlling my thoughts. But there is one thing that I do know with absolute certainty: *I know that I am now having certain thoughts and experiences.* Even if it is nothing but an illusion, I know that I am having the *experience* "fireplace in front of me." I cannot be wrong about that. Similarly, even if an evil spirit is deceiving me, I still know that I am having the *thought* "2 + 3 = 5." I know my own thoughts and experiences, and you know your own thoughts and experiences. That's the one thing we can't be mistaken about.

(2) If it is certain that we have thoughts and experiences, then it is certain that we exist. After all, if we did not exist, we could not be having those thoughts. Descartes expresses this inference as "I think, therefore I am"—or, in the Latin version, *Cogito, ergo sum*—one of the most famous propositions in the history of thought.

(3) Among our ideas is one that stands out, namely, the idea of God. Our other ideas, such as the idea of a fireplace, are ideas of things that might not exist in reality. But the idea of God is different, because it is the idea of a perfect being, and so it is the idea of something that must exist in reality. Why? Because not existing in reality is incompatible with being perfect. Therefore, God must exist. (This is the Ontological Argument, which we discussed in chapter 2.)

(4) We have now established that we exist, along with our thoughts and experiences, and that God, a perfect being, also exists. But God, if he is perfect, cannot be a deceiver. It follows that God could not have made us so that we would be systematically deceived about what the world is like. A perfect, truthful God would design our sense organs and intellect so that we would come to have true beliefs, not false beliefs.

(5) It follows, then, that our senses and our powers of reasoning are reliable sources of knowledge about the world around us.

This argument leaves Descartes with a residual problem: If our faculties were designed and made by a perfectly good creator, why do we sometimes make mistakes? Error, he says, results from human action, not divine action. When we make mistakes, it is because we employ our faculties carelessly, or because other humans set out to deceive us.

Descartes' argument provides an answer to our earlier worries. If there is a perfect God, as it says in step (3), then there is no Evil Demon (or if there is, then the Demon's power to deceive us is kept in check by God). And if, as it says in step (5), our senses and powers of reasoning are reliable, then Idealism should be false, since our senses and powers of reasoning so naturally lead us to believe that physical objects exist. Finally, the dream hypothesis and the brain-in-a-vat hypothesis should not be true in Descartes' world, since a perfect being would protect us from a life of perpetual illusion.

Is Descartes' argument sound? Descartes' reasoning has been analyzed endlessly for the last three-and-a-half centuries. Today in North America there are probably a dozen graduate students writing dissertations about it. One problem is that serious objections have been raised to the Ontological Argument for God's existence. Another problem is that Descartes' procedure is circular: He reasons his way to the conclusion that reasoning can be trusted. Essentially, his argument goes like this: "How do we know that reasoning can be trusted? Because God created our powers of reasoning, and God is not a deceiver. How do we know that? Because we have a chain of reasoning to prove it." Among philosophers, this is known as "the Cartesian Circle." Because of these problems, nobody now thinks that Descartes provided an absolutely certain basis for human knowledge. That goal was too ambitious. Complete certainty, it seems, is beyond human powers.

Even if his argument was faulty, Descartes made a number of lasting contributions. First, he clearly identified the problem. Second, he showed that a theological perspective might provide a solution to that problem: human knowledge might find a secure basis in the existence of an honest deity. It is well known that religion might inform our views on morality, mortality, and the origin of the universe. Surprisingly, Descartes shows that religion might also help explain the basis of knowledge. Indeed, we might say that Descartes presents us with a challenge: If we do *not* assume the existence of God, then how can we solve the problem?

10.5. Direct vs. Indirect Realism

We still haven't solved our central problem. We haven't explained why a belief in physical matter is more reasonable than a belief in Idealism, nor have we warded off Descartes' deceiving Demon or refuted the brain-in-a-vat scenario. Admittedly, our problem has an air of unreality about it. You might think it looks like a problem invented by people who have too much time on their hands. If so, many philosophers agree with you. On their view, the problem arises from a mistake.

So far, our discussion has assumed a particular view of how sense perception works. The view is this:

> When we look at an object, we do not see the object itself. Instead, we are aware of an "experience," or an "idea in our minds," or a "sense-datum," or a "mental representation," or some such. Then we want to infer from these experiences that the object exists. The problem is to explain how this inference is justified.

But, critics say, this account of perception is mistaken. The mistake is saying that, when we look at a tree, we see only some sort of mental image. Instead, *we see the tree.* We see a physical object that exists outside us. We do not "infer" that the tree exists. We see it directly.

Seeing is a way of getting information about the world around us. But it is not a two-step process, in which we first get information about "sense-data" and then move from that to information about the tree. Instead, it is a one-step process of seeing the tree. That's how we know the tree is there. The brain-in-a-vat hypothesis, and the Evil Demon hypothesis, cannot be refuted, but under normal circumstances, we have good reason to reject them—we have direct awareness of the reality they deny.

Of course, we may sometimes be mistaken, but that fact poses no special problem. We discover our mistakes in the same way we learn everything else, by using our senses and our intelligence. I think I see a tree—is it an illusion? I find out by looking more closely, or by trying to touch it, or by asking someone else to check, or by considering whether I have been drinking too much. If I think I might be suffering a hallucination but have no way to check, I may simply suspend judgment. Normally, however, I know I see a tree.

This view is known as Direct Realism. It is contrasted with Indirect Realism, which holds that our immediate object of perception is something mental—our idea of a tree—whereas we are only indirectly aware of the tree itself. Direct Realism appeals to common sense and seems to give a straightforward answer to the science-fiction scenarios. Its defenders include such eminent figures as Ludwig Wittgenstein (1889–1951) and J. L. Austin (1911–1960). But Direct Realism is unsatisfying, for two reasons.

First, Direct Realism doesn't actually help us solve problems like the brain in the vat. We want to be given evidence that we're not brains in vats; we want a reason to believe that we *are* in touch with an external reality. Direct Realism, however, merely asserts that we're in touch with an external reality. And, on the strength of that assertion, it concludes that we *know* we're in touch with an external reality. To borrow a phrase from Bertrand Russell, this solution to the problem has all the advantages of theft over honest toil.

Second, Direct Realism does not fit well with what we know about how the brain processes information. "Seeing" a tree is not a simple matter at all; it is the result of neurological processes that have a complicated structure. Our theory of perception should mesh with our scientific understanding of how this processing works.

10.6. Vision and the Brain

The German philosopher Immanuel Kant (1724–1804) is famous for insisting that perception is not a passive process. The mind does not simply record what passes before it; instead, the mind actively interprets experience according to certain built-in principles. Therefore, what we think of as "simple" perception is actually the result of a complicated interpretation of the sensory data. Today, nobody accepts the details of Kant's account. However, his basic idea is confirmed by current research.

The psychologist Steven Pinker (1954–) writes:

When [organisms] apprehend the world by sight, they have to use the splash of light reflected off its objects, projected as a two-dimensional kaleidoscope of throbbing, heaving streaks on each retina. The brain somehow analyzes the moving collages and arrives at an impressively accurate sense of the objects out there that gave rise to them.

How does the brain do this? Nobody knows for sure, but one leading idea is that the brain makes a number of assumptions about how the "throbbing, heaving streaks" are to be interpreted. Thus, what we see is determined by these assumptions as well as by the streaks. Here are four of those assumptions:

1. Sharp lines are interpreted as boundaries or edges, while enclosed areas of one color are taken to be surfaces.
2. Objects have the simplest shapes consistent with the pattern of light that hits our retinas. Thus, a skinny rectangle is more likely to be a stick than a penny viewed edgewise.
3. Surfaces are assumed to be evenly textured. Gradual changes in surface coloration are therefore interpreted as due to lighting and perspective. For example, if you see a surface covered with rows of dots, and if the dots in succeeding rows seem to be closer and closer together, your brain will interpret this as an effect of perspective. It will "see" the dots as evenly spaced. Likewise, if the surface grows gradually darker from one side to the other, the surface will be perceived as evenly colored, with the shading interpreted as an effect of the lighting.
4. To quote Pinker: "Objects have regular, compact silhouettes, so if Object A has a bite taken out that is filled by Object B, A is behind B; accidents don't happen in which a bulge in B fits flush into the bite of A." Think of a suitcase with a bowl in front of it, so that you can't see the corner of the suitcase. You don't assume that the corner of the suitcase is missing and that the bowl fits neatly into the vacant space. Instead, you assume that the bowl is in front of the suitcase, blocking your view.

These assumptions are what philosophers call *defeasible*—they are correctable in light of further experience. Thus, we might move the bowl and discover that the suitcase really does have a missing corner. Or, if the sticklike object is rotated, it could turn out to be a penny.

A further problem is why we don't perceive the world as a montage of two-dimensional surfaces. Instead, we perceive it as a collection of three-dimensional *objects*. How do we manage that? Psychologist Irving Biederman argues that the brain interprets information from the eyes using a stock of 24 basic three-dimensional shapes, which he calls "geons." Biederman suggests that the geons are the brain's inbuilt device for constructing objects from the data of experience. The geons include such basic units as a sphere, a cube, a cylinder, and a bent tube; and all objects are said to be constructed by combining these basic units. (This will come as no surprise to art students, who traditionally are taught to draw and shade such standard "solids" as a preliminary to tackling more complicated objects.) A bent tube on top of a box is a suitcase. A bent tube on top of a cylinder is a bucket. A bent tube on the side of a cylinder is a cup. And so on. Kant spoke of the mind imposing its forms on experience; according to Biederman, geons are among the forms.

Color, one of the last elements added by the brain, can make a huge difference to our emotions. The neurologist Oliver Sacks (1933–) has studied what happens to people who suffer brain damage that makes them completely color-blind, so that they see only whites, blacks, and greys. For some of these people, vision is not like watching a black-and-white TV—rather, something important is missing along with the colors. One of Sacks's patients, Jonathan I., was a painter who became color-blind after a car accident. His eyes weren't damaged, but the part of his brain that constructs color was. Even in his mind's eye, he could see only blacks, whites, and greys. According to Sacks, Jonathan I. found his new world to be alien, empty, and dead. He avoided other people, who seemed to him "like animated grey statues," and he found food to be disgusting. Even when he closed his eyes, Jonathan I.'s mental image of a tomato looked just as black as its appearance.

Finally, we have two eyes that view the world from slightly different angles, and the brain has a way of combining the information from them to tell us how far away objects are. To us, it may seem obvious that perceiving depth is the purpose of binocular vision. However, this is a recent discovery. Until the nineteenth century, it was thought that having two eyes is simply a by-product of the fact that our bodies are symmetrical; or, it was thought, the second eye may be a spare in case something happens to the first.

It should thus come as no surprise that most of the fibers going to the brain's vision center do not come from the retina. Rather, 80 percent of those fibers come from deep within the brain itself. Our brains work hard to interpret the splashes of light reflected onto our retinas. Are those interpretations arbitrary? Why do we make them? The answer is that the human brain is the product of evolution. We process information in the ways that contributed to the survival of our ancestors, who needed to find food, avoid predators, interact with other members of their species, and otherwise move safely through the world. Thus, we have evolved a perceptual system that is useful for our purposes.

10.7. Conclusion

The commonsense view of perception goes something like this:

> We have experiences such as "seeing a tree" or "hearing a cricket" because our bodies interact with a physical world that includes things like trees and crickets. The world impinges on our sense organs, causing us to have experiences and beliefs that represent the world to us in a fairly accurate way. The physical world exists independent of us—that is, it would exist even if we didn't exist, and it continues to exist even when we are not observing it.

Nothing we've discussed gives us any reason to reject this commonsense view. However, in the previous section, we saw that the brain plays a more active role in perception than common sense might suppose. The brain does not merely "read off" the data of experience coming from our senses; rather, the brain adds to those data and actively interprets them. As one writer put it, "The account of perception that's starting to emerge is what we might call the 'brain's best guess' theory of perception: perception is the brain's best guess about what is happening in the outside world."

According to common sense, Idealism is false: we really do interact with a physical world. Also, common sense holds that our experiences and beliefs "represent the world to us in a fairly accurate way." Thus, common sense rejects the idea that we're being systematically deceived, either by Descartes' Demon or by the scientists who manipulate all the brains in vats. However, these are mere assumptions—the commonsense view offers no argument against Idealism, nor does it give us any reason to believe that we're not being systematically duped. What, then, has become of our attempt to refute these bizarre possibilities? It has failed. We have found no reason at all to believe that we're not living in the Matrix.

CHAPTER 2

God and the Origin of the Universe

I cannot think that this watch exists and has no watchmaker.
—Voltaire, *Les Cabales* (1772)

2.1. Is It Reasonable to Believe in God?

Most Americans believe in God. In fact, according to a recent Gallup poll, 56 percent of Americans say that religion plays a "very important" role in their lives. And when the Pew Research Center conducted polls in different countries, it found the United States to be much more religious than other developed Western nations. In France, only 14 percent say that religion is very important to them. In Great Britain, the figure is 18 percent; in Spain, 21 percent; and in Canada and Germany, 27 percent. However, Indonesians, Pakistanis, and Indians are even more religious than Americans. Thus, in terms of professed religious faith, Americans are "closer to people in developing nations than to the publics of developed nations."

Meanwhile, the Gallup International Millennium Survey asked people in 60 countries whether they believed in God at all. Only 45 percent said they believed in a "personal" God, while another 30 percent said they believed in "some sort of spirit or life force." The Gallup poll found that religious belief is strongest in the elderly and the uneducated and that the rate of belief is highest in West Africa, where Islam dominates. There, 99 percent believe in a personal God. In the United States, the figure is 86 percent, while Europeans "are the most agnostic."

But we want to know more than what people believe—we want to know whether religious beliefs are *true*. Does God exist?

Did he create the universe? Does he listen to prayers? Some people might say that such questions are about faith, and so reason is irrelevant. The pronouncements of Scripture or the Church do not require confirmation by rational argument. It is tempting to let the matter rest there—some choose to believe, others do not, and that's all there is to it. But before reaching that conclusion, we should ask what evidence is available. Can good reasons be given to support belief in God? We should not say that religious belief is "merely" a matter of faith until we are sure that rational arguments cannot be found.

The problem is that God cannot be detected by ordinary means. He cannot be seen or heard or touched, and scientific instruments are useless. Some people say they can sense his presence, but others cannot. This suggests that belief in God is only a matter of inner conviction. Nonetheless, religious thinkers have offered various arguments for the existence of God.

2.2. The Argument from Design

The Argument from Design tries to infer God's existence from the nature of the world around us—the world contains wonders that are best explained by supposing that an intelligent designer created them. As we shall see, this thought can be developed in different ways.

The Wonders of Nature. The world is full of amazing things that we take for granted. Consider, for example, the human eye. It is made of parts that work together in intricate, complicated ways. The eye has an opening through which light enters, while a mechanism makes the opening larger or smaller depending on the amount of light present. The light then passes through a lens that focuses it on a sensitive surface, which in turn translates the patterns into signals that can be transmitted to the brain through the optic nerve. If any detail is changed, the whole process stops working. Imagine that there was no hole in the front of the eyeball, or no lens, or no nerve connecting it to the brain—then everything else would be pointless.

Countless other examples could be given. The plants and animals that populate the earth are all composed of parts that work together beautifully. These living things form a delicate but viable ecosystem. Plants are eaten by animals, who are eaten by other animals, who die and rot and feed the plants. The earth itself, moreover, is exquisitely fitted to support the life on it, being just the right distance from the sun and having just the right temperature, water, and atmosphere. Considering all this, we might wonder whether it could all have arisen by chance. It looks like the work of an intelligent designer.

This line of thought has occurred to many people, but it was William Paley (1743–1805), an Anglican clergyman and teacher at Cambridge University, who developed it most memorably. Paley's favorite example was the eye. Even forgetting about the eye's ingenious construction, consider how it is situated in the head: For protection it is lodged in a deep, bony socket, which protects it with a layer of fat. There are lids to further protect it. Glands are constantly producing a wash to keep the eye moist, without which, once again, the whole contraption would be worthless.

But, one might ask, so what? Having observed these remarkable facts, the argument can continue in two ways.

The Best-Explanation Argument. First, we may note that the wonders of nature require some sort of explanation. How, exactly, did the various parts of the eye come to exist? One possibility is that it all happened by chance—the lens, the optic nerve, the eyelid, and all the rest just happened to spring into being simultaneously. How lucky for us! But that is hard to believe. Yet, if chance is eliminated, what remains? Intelligent design seems to be the alternative. The eye and the other wonders of nature could have been made by God. Thus we have the Best-Explanation Argument:

(1) Either the wonders of nature occurred randomly, by chance, or they are the products of intelligent design.

(2) Intelligent design explains the existence of these things much better than blind chance does.

(3) Therefore, the wonders of nature are best explained as the products of intelligent design.

The Same-Evidence Argument. A different form of the argument appeals to the idea that *we have the same evidence* that the universe was designed by an intelligent creator as we have that other things, such as telescopes, were designed. To make this point, Paley introduced one of the most famous analogies in the history of science, that of the watchmaker.

Suppose we find a watch lying on the ground. If we inspect it, we will conclude that it was designed by an intelligent being. After all, it is made of many small parts that work together to serve a purpose. In Paley's words, "[I]ts several parts . . . are so formed and adjusted as to produce motion, and that motion so regulated as to point out the hour of the day. . . . [T]he inference we think is inevitable [is] that the watch must have had a maker." Thus, from the existence of the watch, we are entitled to infer the existence of a watchmaker. But do we not have exactly the same sort of evidence that the universe was made by an intelligent designer? The universe also consists of "parts framed and put together for a purpose"—namely, the purpose of housing intelligent life. And do we not have the same sort of evidence that some things in the universe—such as the eye, with its parts magnificently aligned for vision—were made by an intelligent designer? The Same-Evidence Argument, then, goes like this:

(1) We conclude that watches were made by intelligent designers because they have parts that work together to serve a purpose.

(2) We have the same evidence that the universe, and some of the natural objects in it, were made by an intelligent designer: they are also composed of parts that work together to serve a purpose.

(3) Therefore, we are entitled to conclude that the universe was made by an intelligent designer.

Hume's Objections. These are impressive arguments, but are they sound? It would be nice if they were, because they would provide rational support for an ancient and satisfying way of understanding the universe. Unfortunately, these arguments are open to some crippling objections made by David Hume (1711–1776), the greatest English-speaking philosopher in history. Hume was a skeptic about religion at a time when skepticism could not be publicly acknowledged. So, he never came right out and said that he didn't believe. Instead, in his book *Dialogues Concerning Natural Religion*, he chipped away at the foundations of belief by exposing weaknesses in various theistic

14   PROBLEMS FROM PHILOSOPHY

arguments. He did not allow *Dialogues Concerning Natural Religion* to be published in his lifetime; it was published after his death, in 1779.

We may begin by noting that the Argument from Design, in all its forms, tries to infer *what causes something* from information about the thing itself. In other words, we are to infer a *cause* from its *effects*. This is a common type of inference, but it is justified only when we have a specific sort of background information.

For example, suppose we are presented with an AIDS patient and asked what caused her disease. We could reply, with confidence, that she must have the human immunodeficiency virus (HIV), and this is the cause. But why are we entitled to infer that? It is because of our past experience. In the past we have seen plenty of cases in which HIV and AIDS were linked. Physicians have treated many patients with AIDS, and in each case the virus was present. Moreover, studies have identified the mechanism that connects HIV and AIDS, and other possible causes have been ruled out. We call upon this background knowledge when we are confronted with a new case of the disease. We know what generally causes AIDS, and we apply this knowledge to specific cases.

Can we infer, in the same way, that an act of divine creation caused the universe to exist? The problem is that we lack the sort of background knowledge that would permit this inference. If we had observed God creating universes many times in the past and had never seen a universe not created by him, then we would be entitled to infer that he must have made our universe. But, in fact, we have no idea what causes universes to come into existence. We are familiar with only one universe; we did not observe its cause; and that's all we know.

The case of the watch is entirely different. When we examine the watch lying on the ground, we have lots of relevant background information. We have seen watches before, and we know that they are made by watchmakers. We can visit the factories where they are produced, and we know the names of the companies that make them. That is why we can say with such confidence that a particular watch must have been made by a watchmaker. This means that the Same-Evidence Argument is fatally flawed. Where causes are concerned, we have vastly more evidence about watches than about universes. Moreover, these observations also cast doubt on the Best-Explanation Argument. Because we have so little experience with the creation of universes, and so little experience with the origin of natural objects, it seems too ambitious to assume that there are just two possibilities: random chance and intelligent design.

But suppose we set these points aside, and we do try to infer how the world came about. If we were serious about this, what would we conclude? What conjecture would seem most reasonable? The idea that the world was made by a single all-powerful, all-good deity would not be very plausible. After all, the world is not perfect. As impressive as the human body is, it is weak and vulnerable to disease. Some people have leprosy or muscular dystrophy. If our eyes were perfect, nobody would need glasses—and some of us, of course, are blind. Taking this into account, it might be more reasonable to conjecture that the world was made by a somewhat inept or malicious world-maker, or that we were made by an apprentice world-maker who had yet to master the craft. Again, we might notice that the world contains elements that work against one another—humans struggle to survive in an environment that is often hostile to them. This might lead us to speculate that the world was designed by a committee of world-makers working at odds with one another. Of course, no one believes such things. But the point is that these conjectures would be at least as reasonable as the idea that the world was made by a perfect God, *if* we were seriously trying to infer the nature of the Creator from the nature of the Creation.

2.3. Evolution and Intelligent Design

As the nineteenth century began, Hume's critique of the Design Argument was well known, but it was not considered decisive. Instead, Paley's argument was widely accepted. In the decades to come, Paley's books, and not Hume's, would be required reading in British universities. The reason for this is clear. The hypothesis of divine creation provided a way to account for the wonders of nature. Hume criticized this hypothesis, but he had nothing to replace it with. Why should people abandon a useful way of understanding the world when they have none better? Thus, the hypothesis of divine creation retained its appeal until an alternative account was found. In 1859, Charles Darwin provided such an account with his Theory of Natural Selection.

16   PROBLEMS FROM PHILOSOPHY

How Natural Selection Works. Many people assume that Darwin was the first person to come up with the idea of evolution, but he was not. In the early nineteenth century, it was already known that the earth is very old and that different kinds of plants and animals have lived at different times. Many people speculated that the appearance and disappearance of all those species might be explained by evolution. But evolution was rejected by scientific thinkers because no one could imagine how one species could change into another. Instead they accepted the theory of *catastrophism*, which holds that a series of great disasters has occurred throughout history—the last, perhaps, being Noah's flood—in which the existing species were destroyed and then replaced by God in a new act of creation. Today catastrophism may seem bizarre, but in the early nineteenth century it was the best theory available, and many scientists accepted it. Then Darwin changed everything by explaining how evolution might take place. The Theory of Natural Selection, which he set out in his book *On the Origin of Species* (1859), supplied the mechanism needed to explain how species evolve over time.

Darwin's genius was in realizing that three well-known facts, taken together, could explain evolutionary change. First, there is the *geometrical increase of populations*. Organisms reproduce in such numbers that, if left unchecked, the members of any one species would soon overrun the earth. (Starting from a few rabbits, there would soon be millions, and shortly thereafter trillions, until we were hip-deep in rabbits.) Second, there is the *heritability of traits*. An organism's descendants tend to resemble it—each individual inherits the characteristics of its parents. Third, there is *variation*. Although individuals resemble their parents, they are not exactly like their parents. There are random small differences between them.

Putting these three facts together, Darwin argued as follows:

(1) Organisms tend to reproduce in such numbers that, if all survived to reproduce again, the members of any one species would overrun the earth. This does not (and could not) happen. No species can continue to multiply unchecked. Each population reaches a certain maximum size, and then its growth stops.

(2) It follows that a high percentage of organisms must die before they are able to reproduce. Therefore,

there will be a "struggle for existence" to determine which individuals live and which die. What determines the outcome of this struggle? What determines which individuals live and which die? There are two possibilities: It could be the result of random causes, or it could be related to the differences between individuals. Sometimes it is random. That is, the reason one organism survives to reproduce while another does not will sometimes be due to causes that have nothing to do with their particular characteristics. One animal may be struck by lightning, for example, while another is not; and this may be mere luck. But sometimes the fact that one individual survives to reproduce while another does not will be due to their different characteristics. It works like this:

- There are differences ("variations") between members of species. Darwin did not know how or why such variations first arise, but today we know it has to do with genetic mutation.

- Some of these differences will affect the organism's relation to its environment, in ways that are helpful or harmful to its chances for survival and reproduction.

- Therefore, because of their particular characteristics, some individuals will be more likely to survive and reproduce than others.

Here are two examples of how this happens. Suppose wolves live in an environment that is growing colder. The wolves with thicker fur will be more likely to survive and reproduce than the wolves with thinner fur. The thicker fur does not appear in response to the weather—it is just a random variation. Nonetheless, it benefits the wolves in the changed environment: wolves with thinner coats will die in the cold, while wolves with thicker coats will survive to reproduce.

Or suppose that a bird like the African finch migrates to an area in which the food supply consists of nuts. Finches with thinner beaks will not be able to crack the nuts; finches with thicker beaks will. The finches with thicker beaks will thus be more likely to survive and reproduce.

(3) When they reproduce, organisms pass on their characteristics to their descendants. Again, Darwin did not know how this happens, but he knew that it does: An organism's offspring will have most of its characteristics. Today, we know this has to do with genes.

(4) Therefore, since the organisms with helpful characteristics survive to reproduce, passing those characteristics on to their children, the characteristics that have "survival value" tend to be more widely represented in future generations, while other characteristics tend to be eliminated from the species. Future generations of wolves and finches will, on average, have thicker fur and thicker beaks.

(5) In this way, a species will be modified—the descendants of the original stock will come to have different characteristics than their ancestors—and, when enough of these modifications have accumulated, we call the result a new species. This is how natural selection works.

The Theory of Natural Selection gave evolution a sound basis, and soon it replaced catastrophism as the dominant account of why different species have lived at different times. It also provided an alternative to the hypothesis of intelligent design, without appealing to blind chance. Rather than explaining the wonders of nature as God's handiwork, we can account for them as the result of natural selection.

Can Natural Selection Account for Biological Complexity?
When Darwin was enrolled at Cambridge University in the late 1820s, all students were required to read Paley's *Natural Theology*. Darwin later wrote in his *Autobiography* that "I was charmed and convinced of the long line of argumentation." At that time, the young Darwin intended to become a clergyman. He abandoned this ambition after completing an around-the-world voyage on the HMS *Beagle* from 1831 to 1835. By 1838 he had formulated the Theory of Natural Selection. After discovering natural selection, Darwin was no longer charmed by Paley's reasoning. Darwin considered the Theory of Natural Selection to be a replacement for the idea that particular aspects of nature were consciously designed. "The old argument of design in nature,"

he said, "which formerly seemed to me so conclusive, fails, now that the law of natural selection has been discovered."

Darwin's views gradually won over the scientific community, but many people have remained skeptical of evolution, or at least skeptical of the idea that evolution eliminates the need for a designer. In the 1970s and 1980s, "creation science" came into vogue in the United States. Creationists accepted the literal truth of Genesis, and they looked for principles to explain the diversity and geographic distribution of life. Activists mounted a campaign to have creation science taught in the public schools as an alternative to evolution, but they failed because creation science was so obviously inadequate. Today the campaign has moved on to a more modest claim, namely, that "intelligent design" should be taught as an alternative to evolution in explaining the origin of species. In 1996, a scientist named Michael J. Behe wrote *Darwin's Black Box: The Biochemical Challenge to Evolution,* in which he argued that some biological systems cannot be the result of natural selection alone because they are "irreducibly complex." Intelligent design, Behe said, is a more plausible explanation of such systems. *Christianity Today* named *Darwin's Black Box* its "Book of the Year."

Why is natural selection supposed to be inadequate? Behe's arguments are too technical in their scientific detail for us to consider. However, it is fair to say that they have not yet convinced many scientists. Typically, the proponents of "intelligent design" point out that complex organs such as the eye are constructed of numerous parts, each of which appears to be useless except when working with the others. How are we to conceive of the evolution of all these parts? Are we to imagine a primitive eye, a primitive tear duct, a primitive lid, and all the rest developing alongside one another? The Theory of Natural Selection says that complex organs are the result of small variations that "add up" to the mature organ after many generations of evolutionary change. But there's a problem with this. Even if the fully developed eye is useful to its possessor, of what use is a half-eye that still has many generations to go before it is complete? Why should a half-eye be "selected for" and preserved for further development? These problems, say the critics, are unsolvable.

But this problem is not new. Darwin himself was aware of it. To address it, he made two points. First, he emphasized that a bit of anatomy may originally be preserved by natural selection for one purpose, but then later, that anatomy might be used for a different purpose. Nature may jury-rig a complex structure out of whatever materials happen to be around. Second, Darwin called attention to what present-day theorists call the *intensification of function*. A biological structure that originally conferred a certain benefit might later confer that same benefit to a much greater degree.

To explain the eye, Darwin said, all we have to imagine is that a nerve only slightly sensitive to light gives an organism some small advantage. Then we can understand the establishment of the first primitive eye. From that simple thing will eventually come our complex eyes.

> In living bodies, variation will cause the slight alterations, generation will multiply them almost infinitely, and natural selection will pick out with unerring skill each improvement. Let this process go on for millions on millions of years; and during each year on millions of individuals of many kinds; and may we not believe that a living optical instrument might thus be formed as superior to one of glass, as the works of the Creator are to those of man?

If the eye itself can be formed in this way, then so can the tear ducts, the eyelid, the bone, and all the rest. Take the lid, for example: Imagine that a primitive eye has been established and that in some organisms a slight variation has resulted in a small fold of skin that somewhat protects it. That variation is random (arising from genetic mutation), but because having this fold of skin makes the primitive eye better, this new feature will be selected for, and further modified, in the usual way. Darwin's analysis has withstood the test of time. Today it forms the basis for scientific thought about these matters.

After Darwin, the Best-Explanation Argument was finally refuted. Hume had pointed out its logical deficiencies, but he could not supply a better way of understanding the apparent design of nature. After taking away design as an explanation, he left nothing in its place. It is no wonder, then, that in the early nineteenth century even the brightest people continued to believe in design. But Darwin did what Hume could not do: He provided a detailed alternative, giving people something different to believe. The Best-Explanation Argument had considered only two ways of explaining the wonders of nature: chance and design. After Darwin, there was a third way.

2.4. The First Cause Argument

Today we know—or at least we think we know—that our universe began in a "Big Bang" almost 14 billion years ago and the earth was formed around 4.5 billion years ago. But what caused the Big Bang? Why is there a universe at all, rather than nothing? This question requires some sort of answer, and here, once again, it may be thought that the hypothesis of divine creation provides the answer. We may conjecture that God was the "first cause" of the universe.

This thought can be developed in at least three ways.

The Idea That God Was the First Cause in the Long Chain of Causes. One line of reasoning appeals to the principle that *everything must have a cause.* My watch was made by watchmakers working with metals extracted from the earth. Where did the watchmakers and the metals come from? The watchmakers came from their parents, while geological processes explain how the metals formed. The chain of causes can be traced back further: Those parents descended from other people, who descended from still other people; the earth itself was formed from matter moving through space; and so on. If we trace everything back far enough, we eventually come to the Big Bang, which in turn must have been caused by something. But, it is said, the chain of causes must stop somewhere; we must come eventually to the First Cause of Everything. The argument goes like this:

(1) Everything must have a cause.

(2) The chain of causes cannot reach back indefinitely; at some point, we must come to a First Cause.

(3) The First Cause we may call "God."

As a statement of faith, this line of thought may be appealing. But if it is meant to prove God's existence, it fails. The main problem is that this reasoning is self-contradictory. It begins by saying that everything must have a cause, but then it goes on to posit the existence of something, God, that has no cause. We must choose: Do we seriously believe that everything must have a cause, or not? If we seriously believe that everything must have a cause, then we must ask what caused God. On the other hand, if we believe that "the chain of causes must stop somewhere," why not say that it stops with the Big Bang? After all, the Big Bang is as far back as science can go, so it is as good a place to stop as any.

Also, this argument doesn't actually tell us that God exists. Its conclusion is merely that we may call the ultimate cause of everything "God." Even if we agree to this, we would not be agreeing that an all-powerful, benevolent deity created the universe. The word "God" might now (for all we know) be the name of an incredibly dense point of mass and energy that preceded the Big Bang. Once this point is appreciated, it becomes clear how misleading it is to use the word "God" in this way.

The Idea That God Caused the Universe "as a Whole" to Exist. We may think of God not as another link in the chain of causes, but as the source of the entire chain itself. The "chain of causes and effects" occurs within the universe. But now we want an explanation of the whole thing—why does the universe exist at all? Science deals only with causes and effects within the universe, and so science cannot tell us why the universe itself exists. For that, we need religion.

Thus, a different form of the argument might be:

(1) Everything that exists within the universe is part of a vast system of causes and effects.

(2) But the universe itself requires an explanation—why does it exist?

(3) The only plausible explanation is that God created it.

(4) Therefore, to explain the existence of the universe, it is reasonable to believe in God.

But this line of thought has its own problems. It is like the Argument from Design in that it attempts to infer the cause of the universe from the existence of the universe itself. The universe exists—that's for sure—but what caused it to come into being? According to step (3), it is most plausible to suppose that God created it. And we may be inclined to agree with this, because of our religious traditions. But Hume's observations are again relevant. To infer the cause of something, we need background information. To infer the cause of a watch, for example, we need information about what kinds of things cause watches to exist. However, we do not have this kind of information about universes. We have never seen a universe being created, and so we can draw no conclusions about what kinds of things create them.

The First Cause Argument is like a lot of philosophical arguments in that we start with a promising idea—in this case, that divine creation might explain the origin of the universe—but run into problems when we try to formulate it into an explicit chain of reasoning. We might now be tempted to give up on the original thought. But before we do, there is one more idea to consider.

2.5. The Idea That God Is a Necessary Being

Peter van Inwagen is a distinguished contemporary philosopher who converted to Christianity as an adult, after he had already done first-rate work in philosophy. Van Inwagen writes that, after he became a Christian, the world seemed very different to him. Before his conversion, he says, "I can remember having a picture of the cosmos, the physical universe, as a self-subsistent thing, something that is just *there* and requires no explanation." But now he can no longer think of the world in that way:

> I can still call the image to mind (I *think* it's the same image), and it still represents the whole world, but it is now associated with a felt conviction . . . that it must depend on something else, something not represented by any feature of the image, and which must be . . . radically different in kind from what the image represents.

If the universe is not "self-subsistent," then it cannot exist by itself. Rather, it must be sustained by something else. But what sort of "something else" could sustain the whole universe? The obvious candidate for this peculiar status is God. God, according to traditional religious thought, is self-sufficient. He is the cause of everything else, but he himself has no cause. He exists eternally, without a cause and without any beginning or end.

What sort of being could be "self-sufficient"? What could be the cause of everything else and yet not itself require a cause? It all sounds very mysterious. But, according to some philosophers, there is a kind of being that could have these characteristics, namely, a *necessary* being. A necessary being is a being that, by its very nature, could not fail to exist. With this idea in mind, we can formulate one final version of the First Cause Argument:

(1) The universe is a dependent thing. It cannot exist by itself; it can exist only if it is sustained by something else—something that is not dependent.

(2) God, a necessary being, is the only thing that is not dependent.

(3) Therefore, the universe is sustained by God.

Does this argument provide good reason to believe that God exists? It is certainly full of puzzling notions. It is puzzling why the universe must be dependent. Why couldn't it exist without being supported by something else? It is puzzling why the universe could be created only by something self-sufficient—why couldn't it be created by something that also depends on something else? But perhaps the most puzzling thing is the notion of a being whose existence is necessary. What sense can be made of this?

The idea of God as a "necessary being" goes back at least as far as St. Anselm (1033–1109), the English monk who is sometimes called the father of medieval scholasticism. Anselm suggested that we conceive of God as "that than which none greater can be conceived." God, in other words, has every possible perfection: He is perfect in knowledge, in power, in goodness, and in every other way imaginable. There is no conceivable way in which he could be better. Anselm maintained, moreover, that this is true *by definition*—trying to imagine God as having an imperfection is like trying to imagine a married bachelor or a triangle with five sides. You can certainly imagine a being *similar* to God that lacks some perfection, but then you are not thinking of God. The concept of God *is* the concept of a perfect being, just as the concept of a bachelor is the concept of an unmarried man or the concept of a triangle is the concept of a three-sided figure.

But Anselm noticed that something remarkable seems to follow from this: If a being is perfect by definition, then that being must exist. After all, if it did not exist, it would not be perfect. (A perfect being that exists is certainly better than the mere idea of a perfect being.) Hence, it is impossible that God not exist, and this is what we mean by a "necessary being." A necessary being *could not fail* to exist. You and I are not necessary beings, because if history had gone differently, then our parents might never have met, and so we might never have existed. But God is different. He had to exist.

This line of reasoning is known as the Ontological Argument. The Ontological Argument is unlike the Argument from Design or the First Cause Argument in that those arguments frequently occur to ordinary intelligent people. Any reflective person, considering the wonders of nature and the origin of the universe, is apt to wonder whether divine creation is needed to explain them. The Ontological Argument, on the other hand, may sound like a philosopher's trick. How can the existence of anything follow from its definition?

Yet the Ontological Argument has persuaded a number of thinkers. René Descartes (1596–1650), whom we will meet again in this book, and Gottfried Wilhelm Leibniz (1646–1716), the philosopher-scientist who along with Newton discovered calculus, both believed that the Ontological Argument is sound. Others, however, have disagreed.

In Anselm's own day, a monk named Gaunilo argued that if this argument proves that God exists, it must also prove that a perfect island exists. Suppose we say that "Islandia" is the name for our concept of a perfect island. Islandia, by definition, is perfect—it cannot be improved on. It follows, then, that Islandia must exist, because if it did not exist, it would not be a perfect island. By the same method, we could prove that a perfect banana exists, or that a perfect man exists. But this, Gaunilo observed, is absurd. Therefore, the Ontological Argument cannot be sound.

Gaunilo's reasoning shows that the Ontological Argument must be mistaken, but it does not explain the nature of the mistake. That was left to Immanuel Kant (1724–1804), considered by many to be the greatest modern philosopher. Kant observed that whether a thing is perfect depends on its properties—whether an island is perfect, for example, depends on its size, its climate, its natural beauty, and so on. Existence, however, is not a property in this sense. Whether such an island exists is a matter of whether anything in the world *has* those properties. Thus, we cannot prove that the island—or anything else—exists just by stipulating that it is "by definition" perfect. The definition of "Islandia" tells us only what Islandia would be like if it existed; it cannot tell us whether there really is such a thing. Similarly, the definition of "God" tells us only what sort of being God would be if he existed. Whether he does exist is another matter.

Conclusion. The whole business of seeking "arguments" for the existence of God might be considered suspect. People rarely believe in God because of arguments. Instead, they simply accept the teachings of their culture, or they believe in God because of some urgent inner conviction. Arguments seem irrelevant.

But arguments are not irrelevant if we want to know what is reasonable to believe. A belief is reasonable only if there is good evidence for its truth. The arguments we have considered are the most impressive attempts yet made to prove the existence of God. But none of these arguments succeed. They all contain flaws, and so they must be judged failures.

The fact that these arguments fail does not mean that God doesn't exist—it only means that these particular arguments do not prove it. There may be other arguments, yet to be discovered, that will be more successful. In the meantime, the idea that God has created the universe may continue to play an important part in the thinking of religious believers. Divine creation may be accepted as part of a satisfying worldview, even if it is not rationally necessary. Like van Inwagen, many thoughtful people may even find this way of thinking irresistible. But, for the present at least, such beliefs cannot be regarded as rationally supported. This conclusion will not surprise those religious people who, in any case, have always regarded their convictions as matters of faith, not logic.

CHAPTER 3

The Problem of Evil

Misery's the river of the world.

—TOM WAITS, *BLOOD MONEY* (2002)

3.1. Why Do Good People Suffer?

Job was prosperous. He owned both land and cattle, and he loved all ten of his children. He was a good man, generous to his neighbors and a leader in the religious life of his community. This combination of riches and virtue made him the most admired person in the region. But then everything went wrong. Foreigners invaded Job's lands, killing his servants and making off with most of his cattle. A fire destroyed the rest, leaving him penniless. Shortly afterward, a storm caused a house to collapse, killing all of his children. Then Job came down with a disease that left him covered with sores. He became so disfigured that people could not recognize him.

When Job's friends came to console him, their pity soon turned to accusation. They were pious, and they thought that Job must have done something to deserve his misfortunes. Surely, they thought, God would not allow Job to suffer unless he deserved it. "Does God pervert justice?" one asked. "God will not reject a blameless man, nor take the hand of evildoers." Another told him, "Know that God exacts of you less than your guilt deserves." But Job knew himself to be guiltless. Still, he could not explain why God had abandoned him.

This story is recounted in the Book of Job, an ancient Jewish writing that is included in the Christian Bible. It is the earliest document we have in which the problem of evil is clearly posed. Of course, the existence of evil is not a "problem" if one takes a nonreligious view of the world. From a secular point of

27

view, it is not hard to explain why bad things happen. The world isn't designed for our benefit. Lightning causes fires, geological forces cause earthquakes, and microbes cause disease. If we happen to be in the way, it's just our bad luck. This explains part of Job's suffering, and human viciousness explains the rest. From a secular standpoint, there is no mystery here, for we do not expect the world to be fair. Disaster strikes the righteous and the wicked alike. We may not like it, but that's the way life is.

The problem arises when we think of the world as under the control of God. God, by definition, is all good, all knowing, and all powerful. An all-good being would not want bad things to happen. He would not want children to get leukemia, or floods to destroy cities, or terrorists to kill the innocent. Instead, he would want to stop such things from happening. And he could, because he's all powerful. Why, then, do terrible things happen?

Philosophers distinguish the *logical* problem of evil from the *evidentiary* problem. The logical problem is that God and evil appear to be incompatible: If God existed, then he would create a perfect world; he would tolerate no imperfections. Yet our world does contain imperfections. So, God does not exist. That argument, however, contains a questionable assumption: that God would create a perfect world. Instead, God might have a good reason to allow some evil to exist. Maybe we can figure out what that reason is, or maybe not. But merely pointing out that there *might* be a reason allows us to say that belief in God is logically consistent with belief in evil.

The evidentiary problem, however, would remain. The evidentiary problem is that, even if God and evil are logically compatible, the existence of evil is nonetheless *strong evidence* that God does not exist. Suppose we find someone's fingerprints on a murder weapon—this is strong evidence that he committed the crime, even if it is logically possible that he was framed. Pending further investigation, the fingerprints make it *likely* that he is the killer. They point in his direction. In the same way, the existence of evil might count against belief in God, even if it does not conclusively prove that God doesn't exist. The fact that there is *so much* evil in the world makes the existence of God seem even less likely.

This is the single biggest problem for religious belief. It is certainly the problem that worries religious people the most. Thus, religious thinkers have tried for centuries to answer Job's question: Why would God let terrible things happen?

3.2. God and Evil

Many distinguished philosophers have defended orthodox religious belief. For the first 1600 years of the Christian era, almost every important philosopher accepted a theistic worldview and worked within it. Following the Enlightenment (1660–1789), however, educated people were drawn to the worldview of modern science, and they began to develop more secular ways of understanding the world. Today philosophical inquiry is generally conducted independently of religion.

In the 1960s, however, religious thought began to make a comeback in philosophical circles. Alvin Plantinga, a Christian philosopher who now teaches at the University of Notre Dame, was an early leader in this movement. Plantinga distinguishes two kinds of theistic response to the problem of evil, a *defense* and a *theodicy*. A defense is a demonstration that the existence of God is logically consistent with the existence of evil. A defense does not pretend to reveal God's actual plan for creation. But it does aim to show that theists who acknowledge the existence of evil are not guilty of a logical contradiction. A theodicy, on the other hand, is more ambitious. A theodicy attempts to "justify the ways of God to man" by explaining how evil fits into God's actual plan for the world. Plantinga does not believe we can provide a theodicy, because we do not know the mind of God. But, he says, a theodicy is not necessary. A defense is all that is needed to permit religious people to continue in their faith.

The problem with this distinction is that a defense requires too little and a theodicy requires too much. As we have seen, a defense is easy to provide—we can simply point out that God might have a reason for permitting evil, even if that reason is unknown to us. It might be all right to stop here if we were concerned only with defending religious belief from the charge of inconsistency. But we are also concerned with the broader question of what belief is reasonable. Does the existence of so much evil make it *unreasonable* to believe in God? Is the existence of so much evil strong evidence against belief in God? To solve this problem, we need more than a mere "defense," but may not need a full-blown theodicy. Instead, we can look for something in between. We need a plausible account of why an all-powerful, perfectly good God might permit great evils, even if we cannot be sure it is God's own reason.

Such accounts have been offered. Five major ideas have been advanced to explain why God might allow evil to exist. We will consider them one at a time.

The Idea That Pain Is Necessary as Part of the Body's Warning System. "Evil" might seem to be a mysterious notion, and it may be difficult to say exactly what evil is. But it is easy to give examples of bad things. The most obvious examples involve pain. Physical pain—especially intense, prolonged pain—is among the worst things in life, and torturers who deliberately inflict such pain are despicable people. But is God among the torturers? Consider a baby born with epidermolysis bullosa, a genetic skin disease that causes blistering all over the body, so that the baby cannot be held or even lie on its back without pain. If God created the world and everything in it, then he created epidermolysis bullosa, and he left babies vulnerable to it. What justification could there be for this?

It may be pointed out that pain has a purpose: It is part of the body's warning system. Pain alerts us to danger. When you twist your arm, it hurts, telling you not to twist it any further. And later, if your arm is still sore, the soreness tells you to leave your arm alone while it heals. Thus, if you could not feel pain, you would be much worse off. In fact, there are people born insensitive to pain, and they typically lead short and tragic lives. Similar observations hold true of other unpleasant experiences, such as fear. Fear motivates you to withdraw from danger. Faced with an angry grizzly bear, it's good to be afraid. So, it may be said, God has given us pain and fear for our own good.

This argument is persuasive as far as it goes, but it does not solve our problem. The trouble is that pain and fear are imperfect mechanisms for danger avoidance. They do not look like they were devised for this purpose by a perfect God. Sometimes we need a warning, but there is no pain. Carbon monoxide poisoning can sneak up on us without warning. Eating ice cream should be painful for the obese, but it is not. At other times, people suffer terribly even though they cannot improve their situation. The pain that accompanies advanced cancer of the throat may tell us that something is wrong, but the information does us no good, and so the victim suffers needlessly. At still other times, pain may be so great that it is debilitating. Then it may hinder us from escaping, rather than helping: A solitary hiker who breaks his leg in the wilderness may die because he cannot drag the broken limb back to civilization. These facts do not fit the hypothesis that God has created pain for our protection. Pain looks more like the product of a hit-or-miss process of evolution than like the work of a perfect designer.

Finally, even if it is a good thing that we can feel pain, this does not explain why God creates *sources* of pain such as epidermolysis bullosa. A mother who asks why God allows her baby to have this disease can hardly be answered by pointing out that pain is part of the baby's warning system. What needs explaining is why the baby's system is being attacked in such a cruel way.

The Idea That Evil Is Necessary So That We May Better Appreciate the Good. St. Augustine (A.D. 354–430) observed that if nothing bad ever happened, then we could not know and appreciate the good. The point is partly logical and partly psychological. Logically, without the concept of evil, there could be no conception of goodness, just as there could be no notion of tallness without a notion of shortness. We could not even know what goodness *is* if we did not have evil for comparison. Moreover, psychologically, if we never suffered, we would take good things for granted and enjoy them less. How could we recognize and enjoy health if there were no disease? Thus, it is foolish to wish for a world that contains only good things.

But even if this is true, it explains only why God might permit *some* evil to exist. We might indeed need a few bad things to happen once in a while, just to remind us how fortunate we are. But it does not explain why there is so *much* evil in the world. The world contains vastly more evil than is necessary for an appreciation of the good. If, say, only half the number of people died every year of cancer, that would be plenty to motivate the appreciation of health. And because we already have cancer, we don't really need epidermolysis bullosa, much less AIDS, muscular dystrophy, cerebral palsy, spina bifida, diphtheria, Ebola, heart disease, diabetes, Alzheimer's, bubonic plague, and a thousand other ailments.

The Idea That Evil Is Punishment for Wrongdoing. Job's friends believed he must have done something to merit his suffering, because a just God "will not reject a blameless man." Thus, they concluded, Job must have deserved what he got.

The idea that evil is punishment for wrongdoing goes back to the creation story in Genesis, which says that humans originally inhabited a world without evil. But the first humans, Adam and Eve, rebelled against God and as a result were cast out of paradise. The idea expressed in this story is not that you and I are still being punished for Adam and Eve's wrongdoing. That would obviously be unfair. The point is that we are all sinners, and our existence in a world of evil is somehow explained by that fact. We suffer because we bring it on ourselves.

What are we to make of this? It would make sense if there were some correlation between one's moral character and how one fares in life. If evil is punishment for sin, we should expect the worst sinners to suffer the worst disasters. But no such correlation exists. Disaster strikes the righteous and the wicked alike, without apparent regard for their virtue. Some of the best people get Parkinson's disease, while some of the worst people enjoy good health.

And what about innocent babies, who sometimes have terrible diseases and die horribly? The doctrine of original sin was introduced into Christian thought partly to deal with this problem. According to that doctrine, we are all born in sin, so even babies are sinners. But it would be absurd to conclude from this that a newborn baby deserves to have epidermolysis bullosa.

The deep problem with using the concept of sin in this way is that it separates sinfulness from what a person actually does. In the ordinary moral sense, what a person deserves depends on his or her behavior. If you deserve ill, you must have done something to deserve it. No doubt all of us have behaved badly at one time or another, so perhaps each of us deserves some degree of punishment. But we don't deserve a horrible disease unless we have done something pretty awful, and a baby hasn't done anything bad at all. Therefore, while this conception of "sin" might have religious significance, it has little to do with moral desert. As Job knew, not all calamities are deserved.

3.3. Free Will and Moral Character

The ideas we have considered so far—that pain is part of the body's warning system, that evil is necessary for appreciating the good, and that evil is punishment for wrongdoing—are unconvincing. But two other ideas are more promising. Together, they make up the most plausible theistic response to the problem of evil.

The Idea That Evil Is the Result of Human Free Will. God could have made the world, it is said, without people in it. It could have been a beautiful place, with sunsets and waterfalls, with daffodils and butterflies, and God could have been pleased with it. But God went one step further and chose to include us as well. What difference did that make? Humans are not just another kind of animal. We are moral agents, able to choose what sorts of persons we'll be, and so we're responsible for our choices. We are capable of love and friendship, and we can envision and accomplish great things. Thus, without human beings the world would be a poorer place. That is why humanity was part of God's plan—or at least why God might have chosen to create us.

But there is a catch: In order to make us moral agents, rather than mere robots, God had to endow us with free will. Freedom makes humans special. In giving us the power of free choice, however, God had to allow that we might sometimes choose badly. He could not have given us free will and at the same time fixed it so that we could never do wrong—we might then have the appearance of free will, but we would not have the real thing.

The result is that human beings have the power to choose evil, and sometimes we do. Therefore, in addition to love, kindness, sympathy, and heroism, humans also bring to the world murder, cruelty, rape, and war. But God is not responsible for that; we are. God is responsible for the overall design of the world and for creating us. His creation is good. Our contribution to it, however, is not always good.

This line of thought is called the Free Will Defense. The Free Will Defense shows that the best world God could have created might contain evil, because the best world might include creatures with free will. Compare:

(a) A world without humans in it, which would not include any of the bad things people do, but would

> also not contain any of the results of human con-
> sciousness, creativity, and virtue

(b) A world with humans in it, which would include
human wickedness but also the good things that humanity brings

If you think that (b) is better than (a), then perhaps the best
world God could have created would have evil in it. This vin-
dicates the perfect goodness of God. After all, we could not
expect more of him than to create the best world possible.

Still, this cannot solve the problem completely. We need
to distinguish two kinds of evil, *moral evil* and *natural evil*. Moral
evil is the evil that people cause by their own actions—murder,
rape, war, and so on. Natural evil, on the other hand, is the
evil that human beings do not cause—disease, earthquakes,
droughts, floods, and other natural disasters. Humans may be
responsible for babies born addicted to narcotics, but we are
not to blame for babies born with epidermolysis bullosa. Thus,
even if the Free Will Defense explains why God would allow
moral evil, it does nothing to explain why he would create natural evil. Therefore, it can be only part of the story.

**The Idea That Evil Is Necessary for the Development of Moral
Character.** Suppose that, at the beginning of time, God decided
to make a world that included human beings, with all the capacities of thought and action that make us who we are. This decision would restrict the kind of world God could make, because
the world would have to be suitable for creatures like us. What
sort of world would that be? What sort of environment would
allow us to grow and develop as human beings?

Imagine a world that was "perfect" in the ordinary sense.
In this world, the temperature would be a balmy 72°F year-
round, and nothing bad would ever happen—there would be
no destructive earthquakes, fires, or floods and no diseases.
There would be no dangerous predators. Moreover, there
would be no hunger. Every tree would bear abundant fruit.
Everyone would live to a ripe old age in perfect health, and
everyone would enjoy life. The environment would be beautiful in a way that we never grow tired of.

You might ask, If God is perfectly good, why didn't he create that sort of world? The answer is that if we lived in *that* sort

of world, we would not be the creatures we are. In a "perfect" world there would be no problems to overcome, and thus no occasion for the development of moral character. There would be no courage, because there would be no dangers to face. There would be no helpfulness or generosity, because no one would need help. All the other virtues—such as kindness, compassion, perseverance, and creativity—would also go by the wayside, because we develop such qualities only by striving against adversity. If we lived in a perfect environment, there would be no work to be done. We would be slugs—slugs who enjoy life, but slugs nonetheless.

Thus, we have a plausible explanation for natural evil: In order to create human beings as creatures with moral character, God had to place us in an environment in which those qualities could be developed. That means an environment with problems to be solved and evils to be overcome. The world that we actually inhabit seems well suited for the development of people like us.

A Complete Account? The most plausible response to the problem of evil combines the Free Will Defense with the idea that evil is necessary for an environment in which human beings can develop and flourish. The former explains moral evil, while the latter explains natural evil. Together, they seem to give a more or less complete account of the evils we face. They explain why a perfectly good, all-powerful God might have created a world like the one we actually inhabit. We need not pretend that this account is a "theodicy" in Plantinga's sense—perhaps God had other purposes in mind, which we are ignorant of. But this account does seem to be the best available way to square the hypothesis of God with the existence of evil.

The picture may be rounded out by adding another idea, namely, that human life as we know it is a mere prelude to the eternal life we will enjoy after we die—or rather, after the bodies we inhabit die. As Peter van Inwagen (1942–) puts it:

> Every human being has an eternal future (and, therefore, the human species has an eternal future). We are now living, and have been living . . . within a temporary aberration in human history, an aberration that is a finite part of an eternal whole. When God's plan of atonement comes to fruition, there will never again be undeserved suffering

or any other sort of evil. The "age of evil" will eventually
be remembered as a sort of transient "flicker" at the very
beginning of human history.

If, indeed, the evil that concerns us is only a "transient flicker"
in human history, then the problem does not seem nearly so
pressing.

Should we be content with this and conclude that the
problem of evil has been overcome? That is different from asking whether we actually believe the theistic story. We are discussing whether the existence of evil is evidence against God's
existence. If evil can be justified within a theistic framework,
then even a nonbeliever should agree that the problem of evil
has been solved.

But three problems stand in the way of such a conclusion. The first has to do with moral evil. The Free Will Defense says that God wants us to be free, so he tolerates the
bad effects of human misconduct. This might explain why
God doesn't step in to prevent small offenses—perhaps those
things should be allowed to occur. But why wouldn't God intervene when people are about to do something awful, like
abuse an innocent child? It is not plausible to say, "Interven-
ing would turn the attacker into a robot" or "Respecting the
abuser's free will is more important than protecting the child."
We would not accept those excuses from a police officer who
passively witnessed the crime, so why should we offer those
excuses on God's behalf? The Free Will Defense explains why
God doesn't intervene all the time, but it doesn't explain why
God allowed the Holocaust or why God allows isolated cases
of extreme cruelty.

The second problem has to do with the theist's explanation of natural evil. The need to develop moral character
might explain why there is *some* evil in the world, but there
is far more evil than is necessary for such a purpose: There
is stunning, overpowering misery that crushes the life out of
people. If we already have AIDS, muscular dystrophy, cerebral
palsy, and spina bifida, why do we also need malaria, tubercu-
losis, and Ebola? If the people of Haiti are already poor and
hungry, why do they need an earthquake on top of it? Nothing
in our account addresses why there is *so much* suffering caused
by natural events.

Consider the true story of:

a man who drove a cement mixer truck. He came home one day for lunch; his three-year-old daughter was playing in the yard, and after lunch, when he jumped into his truck and backed out, he failed to notice that she was playing behind it; she was killed beneath the great dual wheels.

If this man were told the story about free will and character development, he might find it unconvincing, not because he is blinded by grief and guilt, but because he hasn't been told why *this* sort of thing must happen, in addition to all the other troubles that plague us. The amount of evil in the world could be reduced by two-thirds, and there would still be more than we could handle.

The third problem has to do with nonhuman animals. The traditional debate about evil has centered on human beings. But human life and history are only a small part of nature and its history. Countless animals suffered terribly in the millions of years that preceded the emergence of *Homo sapiens,* and none of the ideas we have been considering address their suffering. Animals are not sinners, they do not have "free will," they do not develop moral character, and they are not going to heaven. What about them? Charles Darwin (1809–1882) made this point forcefully:

> That there is much suffering in the world no one disputes. Some have attempted to explain this in reference to man by imagining that it serves for his moral improvement. But the number of men in the world is as nothing compared with that of all other sentient beings, and these often suffer greatly without any moral improvement. A being so powerful and so full of knowledge as God who could create the universe, is to our finite minds omnipotent and omniscient, and it revolts our understanding to suppose that his benevolence is not unbounded, for what advantage can there be in the sufferings of millions of the lower animals throughout almost endless time?

We are left, then, with this conclusion. Our survey of ideas about how to reconcile God with evil has turned up various thoughts that might be useful. But none of them succeed in reconciling the existence of God with the amount of suffering in the world. All the gratuitous, pointless evil that exists not only poses a serious problem for the believer. It is also a reason why someone who is considering whether to believe in God might decide not to.

CHAPTER 8

The Case against Free Will

A small part of the universe is contained within the skin of each of us. There is no reason why it should have any special physical status because it lies within this boundary.
—B. F. SKINNER, *ABOUT BEHAVIORISM* (1974)

8.1. Are People Responsible for What They Do?

In 1924, two Chicago teenagers, Richard Loeb and Nathan Leopold, kidnapped and murdered a boy named Bobby Franks just to prove they could do it. The crime caused a sensation. Despite the brutality of what they had done, Leopold and Loeb did not appear to be especially wicked. They came from rich families and were both outstanding students. At 18, Leopold was the youngest graduate in the history of the University of Chicago, and at 19, Loeb was the youngest graduate ever from the University of Michigan. Leopold was about to enroll at Harvard Law School. How could they have committed a senseless murder? Their trial would receive the same level of attention that the O. J. Simpson trial did 70 years later.

The parents hired Clarence Darrow, the most famous lawyer of the day, to defend them. Darrow was a champion of unpopular causes—he had defended labor organizers, communists, and a black man accused of killing a member of a racist mob. In 1925, in his most celebrated case, he would defend John Scopes of Tennessee from the charge that he had taught evolution in a high school classroom. Darrow was also the country's best-known opponent of the death penalty. In 1902, he had been invited by the warden to give a talk to the inmates of the Cook County Jail in Chicago, and he told the prisoners:

> I really do not in the least believe in crime. There is no such thing as a crime as the word is generally understood. I do not believe there is any sort of distinction between the real moral conditions of the people in and out of jail. One is just as good as the other. The people here can no more help being here than the people outside can avoid being outside. I do not believe that people are in jail because they deserve to be. They are in jail simply because they cannot avoid it on account of circumstances which are entirely beyond their control and for which they are in no way responsible.

These ideas would figure prominently in Darrow's defense of Leopold and Loeb.

The public wanted blood. As the trial began, the *Chicago Evening Standard* carried this headline:

DARROW PLEADS FOR MERCY: MOBS RIOT
BAILIFF'S ARM BROKEN AND WOMAN FAINTS AS FRENZIED MOB
STORMS PAST GUARDS; JUDGE CALLS FOR 20 POLICE; FEARS SOME
WILL BE KILLED

Leopold and Loeb had already admitted their guilt, so Darrow's job was just to keep them from the gallows. There would be no jury. The judge would listen to the lawyers' arguments and then decide whether the defendants would hang.

Darrow spoke for more than 12 hours. He did not argue that the boys were insane; nevertheless, he said, they were not responsible for what they had done. Darrow appealed to a new idea that psychologists had proposed, namely, that human character is shaped by an individual's genes and environment. He told the judge, "Intelligent people now know that every human being is the product of the endless heredity back of him and the infinite environment around him."

> I do not know what it was that made these boys do this mad act, but I do know there is a reason for it. I know they did not beget themselves. I know that any one of an infinite number of causes reaching back to the beginning might be working out in these boys' minds, whom you are asked to hang in malice and in hatred and injustice, because someone in the past sinned against them.

Psychiatrists had testified that the boys lacked normal feelings, because they showed no emotional reaction to what they had done. Today a psychiatrist might say that Leopold and Loeb suffered from "antisocial personality disorder," commonly known as "sociopathy" or "psychopathy." Darrow seized upon this idea:

> Is Dickie Loeb to blame because out of the infinite forces that conspired to form him, the infinite forces that were at work producing him ages before he was born, that . . . he was born without [the right kind of emotions]? If he is, then there should be a new definition for justice. Is he to blame for what he did not have and never had?

Darrow portrays Loeb as having had a childhood bereft of the affection that boys need, spending his days studying and his evenings secretly reading crime stories, fantasizing about committing the perfect crime and fooling the cops. Leopold, meanwhile, was weak and without friends. He grew up obsessed with Nietzsche's philosophy of the "superman," disdaining other people and desperately wanting to prove his own superiority. Then the two boys found one another and committed the crime. But they were just playing out the hand nature dealt them. "Nature is strong and she is pitiless," Darrow concluded. "She works in her own mysterious way, and we are her victims. We have not much to do with it ourselves."

The judge deliberated for a month and then sentenced Leopold and Loeb to life in prison. Twelve years later, Richard Loeb was attacked and killed by another prisoner. For his part, Nathan Leopold spent 34 years behind bars. During that time, he taught other prisoners, volunteered for malaria testing, ran the prison library, and worked in the prison hospital. After his release on parole, he moved to Puerto Rico, where he continued his lifelong effort to "become a human being again," largely through jobs that involved helping others. He died in 1971.

8.2. Determinism

Clarence Darrow was the first lawyer to use the defense that people are never responsible for their actions, because their actions are caused by forces beyond their control. However, Darrow was not the first person to doubt that we choose our own destinies.

Aristotle worried that the laws of logic might imply that we have no choice about what we do. Every proposition, he reasoned, must be either true or false. So at this moment it is either true or false that you will drink a Diet Coke tomorrow. If it is true, then there is nothing you can do to prevent it—after all, *it will happen.* If it is false, then there is nothing you can do to make it happen, for *it will not happen.* Either way, the future is fixed, and you cannot change it. This became known as the problem of Fatalism. Theologians from St. Augustine onward realized that the assumption of God's omniscience creates a similar difficulty. If God knows everything, he knows what you will do tomorrow. But if God already knows what you will do, then you cannot do otherwise.

Fatalism is a serious problem, but it is not the biggest challenge to human freedom. A greater threat is posed by Determinism, which was known in the ancient world but came into its own with the rise of modern science. To say that a system is deterministic means that everything that happens in it stems from prior causes. Once the causes occur, the effects must follow, given the surrounding circumstances and the Laws of Nature. For example, you expect the electrical devices in your home to be deterministic systems. If your reading lamp goes out, you expect there to have been a cause: the filament in the bulb burned out, or your little brother pulled the plug out of the socket, or something. If you could not fix the problem, and the repairman said, "It just happened, for no reason," that would violate your conception of how things work.

With the rise of modern science, it became common to think of the whole universe as one giant deterministic system. Nature consists of particles that obey the laws of physics, and everything that happens is governed by the unchanging laws of cause and effect. This idea was vividly expressed by the French mathematician Pierre-Simon Laplace (1749–1827), who said that if a supremely intelligent observer knew the exact location and velocity of every particle in the universe and all the laws of physics, he could predict with certainty every future state of the universe. Nothing would surprise him; he would know everything before it happened. As Laplace knew, we cannot actually make such predictions, but only because we lack the necessary information.

The universe includes us. We are part of nature, and what happens inside our skins is subject to the same physical laws as everything else. The movements of our arms, legs, and tongues are triggered by events in our brains, which in turn are caused by other physical occurrences. Thus, Laplace's perfect observer could predict our actions in the same way that he predicts everything else. In fact, by tracing the causes far enough back, he could have predicted whether you will drink a Diet Coke tomorrow even before you were born. It may *seem* to us that we make our choices freely and spontaneously, but Laplace argued that our "freedom" is only an illusion created by our ignorance. Because we aren't aware of what causes our behavior, we assume that we act freely.

What, exactly, are the underlying causes of our behavior? As Darrow observed, the "ultimate" causes may stretch far back in time. But the immediate causes are events in our brains. Neurological events cause both our mental states to occur and our bodies to move. This last claim is not mere speculation. Brain surgery sometimes takes place under only a local anesthetic, so the patient can tell the surgeon what he or she is experiencing as various parts of the brain are probed. This technique was pioneered more than a half-century ago by Dr. Wilder Penfield, who described it in his book *The Excitable Cortex in Conscious Man* (1958). Neurosurgeons have been using Penfield's technique ever since. They know that if you probe in one place, the patient will feel a tingle in her hand; and if you probe in another place, the patient will smell garlic. In one patient, probing in still another place made her hear a song by Guns n' Roses.

Actions can also be induced by electrical stimulation of the brain. Jose Delgado (1915–), a Yale University scientist, discovered that stimulating various regions of the brain could cause all sorts of bodily motions, including frowning, the opening and closing of the eyes, and movements of the head, arms, legs, and fingers. When he first tried this using cats and monkeys, Delgado noticed that the animals showed no surprise or fear when their bodies moved. Apparently, they experienced the movements as voluntary. In one instance, stimulating a monkey's brain caused the monkey to get up and walk around. The effect was repeated several times, and each time the animal strolled around without surprise or discomfort, as if it had just decided to take a walk.

Some philosophers would say that Delgado's technique produced only bodily movements, not actions, because actions involve reasons and decisions. But there is more. When Delgado tried his experiment on humans, not only did they act out the movements without surprise or fear, but they also produced reasons for them. In one subject, electrical stimulation of the brain produced "head turning and slow displacement of the body to either side with a well-oriented and apparently normal sequence, as if the patient were looking for something." This was repeated six times over two days, confirming that the stimulation was actually producing the behavior. But the subject, who did not know about the stimulation, considered the activity spontaneous and offered reasons for it. When asked "What are you doing?" he would reply, "I am looking for my slippers," "I heard a noise," "I am restless," or "I was looking under the bed."

Are our *decisions* also produced by neural firings? There are some experimental results about this, too, due to the German scientist H. H. Kornhuber. Suppose you sit quietly, and sometime during the next minute you spontaneously move your finger. Subjectively, you may feel certain that the decision to move your finger is entirely within your control. But now suppose we attach some electrodes to your scalp and ask you to repeat the action. A technician watching an EEG (an electroencephalograph) would be able to observe a characteristic pattern of brain activity when you move your finger. The brain activity begins up to one-and-a-half seconds before the movement, and *it begins before you make your decision.* So the technician, watching his monitor, knows that you are going to move your finger before you do. He is, in a small way, like Laplace's perfect observer. Kornhuber first performed this experiment in the 1970s.

8.3. Psychology

It may seem odd that the primary argument against free will appeals to the principles of physics. After all, psychologists, not physicists, study human behavior. So we might wonder what psychology has to say. Do psychological theories about human behavior have room for the notion of free will, or do they support Determinism?

100   PROBLEMS FROM PHILOSOPHY

Before turning to psychology, however, let me mention some of the ways in which our commonsense understanding of human beings already contains elements favorable to Determinism. Each of us was born to particular parents at a particular time and place, and only a little thought is needed to realize that if those circumstances had been different, we would have turned out different. A young man "chooses" to become a stockbroker—is it a coincidence that his father is a stockbroker? What would he choose if his parents were missionaries? What would he have chosen if he had been born into a different culture?

We also know from statistics that social conditions influence us in ways we don't realize. Consider, for example, the names we give to our children. White parents tend to choose different names than black parents. In California in the 1990s, for example, girls named Molly and Amy were overwhelmingly white, while girls named Imani and Ebony were overwhelmingly African-American. Social differences between the white and black communities resulted in different names being popular. Socioeconomic status also influences our naming decisions. Again in California, the most common names given to rich white girls in the 1990s were Alexandra, Lauren, Katherine, and Madison; poor white girls were most often called Amber, Heather, Kayla, and Stephanie. These trends change over time. Sometimes "rich names" become more popular among the poor, which in turn causes the rich to abandon them. Individually, parents may always seem to be making free, independent choices. But when social circumstances change, so does the popularity of the names.

Or consider another example: The United States has the highest rate of imprisonment in the world. Over two million Americans are now in jail or prison, and five million more are on probation or parole. Here are some social factors that have been shown, statistically, to be predictive of criminal behavior: having an uneducated mother, growing up poor, being raised in a single-parent household, and having a teenage mother. Considered as individuals, it may seem that each person "freely decides" to break the law. However, many of these individuals would not have broken the law, had their circumstances been different.

When we set aside statistics and try to understand in more detail why individuals behave as they do, we always seem to wind up with explanations in which "free choice" plays little part. Darrow's explanation of how Leopold and Loeb came to kill Bobby Franks is one example. For another, consider Eric Rudolph, who committed a series of bombings in Georgia and Alabama in the 1990s. I heard one of the explosions from my office—the bomb killed a policeman and critically wounded a nurse at an abortion clinic in Birmingham, Alabama. Rudolph was caught in 2003, and today he is serving five consecutive life sentences.

Why would he have done such a thing? Why did he kill the policeman and maim the nurse in Alabama? We might suppose that Rudolph hated abortion so much that he was willing to use any means to stop it. That may be true, but a lot of people oppose abortion without planting bombs. Why did this particular man turn deadly?

According to *Newsweek* magazine, "He is perhaps best understood as the product of a paranoid fringe of white supremacists, religious zealots and government haters. Rudolph's mind and motives are hard to fathom, but extremism seems to run in the family." When he was 13, Eric's father died, and his family moved from Miami to rural North Carolina. There they lived on a gravel road near a sawmill owner named Tom Branham. Branham, a survivalist who had been arrested on federal weapons charges, took an interest in Eric and his brother Daniel and became a substitute father to the boys. His mother, meanwhile, moved to the Missouri Ozarks to join a community of white separatists. By the time he was in the ninth grade, Eric was writing in a class paper that the Holocaust never happened, using as his "research" pamphlets issued by hate groups. As much as we might detest what Eric Rudolph became, it is hard to believe that the little boy had a chance.

Classical Psychology. The effort to understand human behavior naturally leads us to consider deterministic explanations. "He just decided to do it" doesn't sound like any explanation at all. Thus, Determinism is a hard-to-avoid by-product of the search to explain behavior. As B. F. Skinner (1904–1990), a Harvard University psychologist, put it:

> If we are to use the methods of science in the field of human affairs, we must assume that behavior is lawful and determined. We must expect to discover that what a man does is the result of specifiable conditions and that once

these conditions have been discovered, we can anticipate
and to some extent determine his actions.

As the science of psychology has developed, one theory after
another has competed for acceptance. But none of them has
had much use for "free will."

For most of the twentieth century, Behaviorism and Freud-
ianism were the most popular theories among psychologists.
Freud sought to understand human conduct by identifying the
unconscious motives of action. Conscious processes of thought
and deliberation are, on his view, only rationalizations for
deeper forces hidden within the psyche. Long-forgotten events
of infancy and early childhood have given each of us unconscious desires and impulses that control us as adults. For example, a woman has a series of relationships with abusive men.
Each time she gets rid of one, she vows never to make that mistake again; but she does, over and over. How can she keep doing
this? She appears to choose freely each time she begins a new
relationship, but really she does not. She has a masochistic personality, formed as a child when she was battered by an abusive
father; now, as an adult, she helplessly reenacts her relationship
with her father again and again. She will not be able to break
the pattern until she confronts her repressed memories and
feelings about her father, possibly after years of psychoanalysis.

The behaviorists would have none of this. On their view,
unconscious thoughts play no part in explaining behavior. In
fact, no thoughts of any kind do. Instead, a person's behavior is explained by the process of conditioning that produced
that behavior. We tend to repeat behavior for which we are re-
warded, and we tend not to repeat behavior when we are punished. Suppose you get an electric shock every time you touch a
fence; you will soon stop touching it. Or suppose that a child is
fed when he says "please" and not fed when he says nothing. He
will soon be saying "please" whenever he is hungry. These are
simple examples, but the principle is supposed to be the same
for all behavior. In theory, everything we do can be explained
as a response to prior conditioning, including our proudest
and noblest actions as well as our most shameful ones.

Is "Character" a Matter of Luck? When we reflect on other
people's misfortunes, we sometimes think, "There but for the
grace of God go I." Are most of the moral differences between

people a matter of luck? Some of the most famous experiments in social psychology suggest that any of us might behave badly if we were unlucky enough to be in the wrong circumstances.

In one experiment, Philip Zimbardo and his colleagues set up a simulated prison in the basement of a Stanford University building. Twenty-four volunteers were assigned to be either guards or prisoners. The experiment was supposed to last two weeks, but it had to be called off after five days because the "guards" treated the "prisoners" so brutally.

In another study, Stanley Milgram asked volunteers to operate a device that administered increasingly severe electric shocks to someone in the next room. The person in the other room was supposed to be "learning" by being punished for giving the wrong answers to questions. (He was, in fact, an actor who was only pretending to be shocked.) Milgram was surprised to discover that every single volunteer was willing to continue shocking the other person even when the levels were labeled as extremely dangerous and the other person could be heard crying and begging the volunteer to stop.

When people hear about these experiments, they invariably feel that *they* would not have acted so badly. This feeling is hard to avoid, yet the participants in the experiments were ordinary people like you and me. Zimbardo comments that, after the guards-and-prisoners experiment was over, the "prisoners" insisted that they would not have been so abusive if they had been guards. But there was no difference between those who were made guards and those who were made prisoners—the assignment was random. The natural conclusion is that the only difference between them was in their circumstances. Apparently, all of us—or at least the great majority of us—have the inner capacity to behave badly if we are in the wrong circumstances.

One other study deserves mention: the "Good Samaritan" experiment of J. M. Darley and C. D. Batson. In Luke's gospel, the Good Samaritan is presented as a model of decent behavior:

> "And who is my neighbor?"
> Jesus replied, "A man was going down from Jerusalem to Jericho, and he fell among robbers, who stripped him and beat him, and departed, leaving him half dead. Now by chance a priest was going down the road; and when he saw him, he passed by on the other side. So likewise a

104   PROBLEMS FROM PHILOSOPHY

Levite, when he came to the place and saw him, passed by on the other side.

"But a Samaritan, as he journeyed, came to where he was; and when he saw him, he had compassion and went to him and bound his wounds, pouring on oil and wine; then he set him on his own beast and brought him to an inn, and took care of him. And the next day he took out two denarii and gave them to the innkeeper, saying, 'Take care of him; and whatever more you spend, I will repay you when I come back.' Which of these three, do you think, proved neighbor to him who fell among the robbers?"

He said, "The one who showed mercy on him."

And Jesus said to him, "Go and do likewise."

The traditional interpretation of this story is that the Samaritan was a man of better moral character—he "had compassion," while the priest and the Levite did not. (Samaritans, incidentally, were people of low standing, while priests and Levites played important roles in the Temple.) Is this right? Darley and Batson decided to investigate the circumstances in which we would be Good Samaritans, using Princeton theology students as their subjects.

In the study, the theology students first filled out forms giving information about themselves, including information about their ethical and religious beliefs. Then half of the students were told to prepare a lecture on ethics, and half were told to prepare a lecture on job opportunities. All the students were told to go to another building to give their lectures. Some were told they needed to hurry, while others were told they had plenty of time. It had been arranged that on their way to the other building they would pass by someone slumped in a doorway, obviously in distress. Would they stop to help?

Some stopped and some did not. But it turned out that their ethical and religious views had nothing to do with it, nor did it matter whether they had ethics or job opportunities on their minds. All that mattered was whether they thought they had time to stop. This small change in circumstances determined who would be heroic and who would be heartless.

8.4. Genes and Behavior

There aren't many Freudians or behaviorists around these days. Both theories try to do too much with too little. One limitation is that, by focusing only on childhood and environmental conditioning, neither theory has much use for genetic explanations. Today, researchers believe that our genes are about as important as the environment in shaping our personalities.

Twin Studies. How can we estimate the influence of genes on human behavior? One strategy is to compare identical twins who were separated at birth and raised in different environments. Typically, these are twins who were adopted by different families. Dissimilarities between the twins, as adults, cannot be due to genetic differences—after all, identical twins have the same genes. Similarities between the twins might be due either to genes or to common environmental factors (even different households will have some things in common). Twin studies can give us at least a rough idea of how much influence genes exert.

At the University of Minnesota, there is an ongoing research project, begun in 1979, called the Minnesota Study of Twins Reared Apart. When such twins are located, they are invited to the university for a series of tests. The researchers have found that identical twins reared apart resemble each other very closely. In some cases, the similarities sound like something out of science fiction.

Among those tested were the "Giggle Sisters," both of whom laughed all the time. Both had the habit of pushing at their noses, which they both called "squidging"; both claimed to have weak ankles as a result of falling when they were 15; both had met their husbands at dances when they were 16; and both had worked as polling clerks.

There were also brothers named Jim, who drove the same model car and smoked the same brand of cigarettes. Both had elaborate workshops at home where they made miniature furniture as a hobby. Both liked to leave little love notes for their wives lying around the house. And they had named their sons James Alan and James Allan.

Most remarkable, perhaps, were Jack Yufe and Oskar Stöhr, whose home environments had been exceedingly different. One twin was raised in Trinidad by his Jewish father, the other in Germany by his Nazi grandmother. Oskar was in the Hitler youth; Jack served in the Israeli navy. When reunited, both were wearing rectangular wire-frame glasses and blue two-pocket shirts with epaulets. Both had small mustaches. Both liked to read magazines from back to front, and both flushed toilets before using them. Also, both men liked the same odd practical joke of startling people by sneezing in elevators.

These are great anecdotes, but we can draw no firm conclusions from them. In the first place, an enormous amount of data would have to be gathered and analyzed before we could know what, if anything, to conclude. Take the blue-shirt-with-epaulets story, for example. How many shirts like that were owned by men in the areas where Jack and Oskar lived? What are the chances of two men from those areas wearing that shirt on the same day? Or, more generally, in any group of males drawn from the same population, what are the chances that any two selected at random will be dressed similarly? Most important of all, what are the chances that there will be *some* striking similarity between two such men, even if it is not how they are dressed? Critics have also said that the anecdotes might be exaggerated. Moreover, it turns out that some of the twins had met one another before they were studied in Minnesota. Thus, some of the similarities might have grown out of their interactions.

The researchers do not, however, base their conclusions on such anecdotes. Instead, the reared-apart twins are given standard psychological tests for such traits as flexibility, tolerance, conformity, self-control, conscientiousness, openness, tough-mindedness, social dominance, alienation, authoritarianism, and aggressiveness. And the twins have been found to be remarkably alike in all these ways. They have similar senses of humor and similar levels of optimism or fearfulness. They share (or lack) similar talents, and they have similar mental illnesses and disabilities. On the basis of such studies, researchers have concluded that the major components of our personalities are about 50 percent due to our genes. And our personalities, of course, affect our behavior.

Are Some People Born Bad? Scientists have long known about the connection between biology and violence. Experiments have shown that if a small section of a cat's hypothalamus is removed, the cat will turn savage. Humans with head injuries sometimes experience fits of uncontrollable rage. Meanwhile, for people who are "naturally" prone to violence, effective treatments include lithium and beta-blockers, which act on the brain. The genes–neurology–violence connection was further confirmed in 1995 when geneticists discovered that turning off the gene responsible for producing nitric oxide—a chemical in the brains of both mice and humans—causes normally sociable mice to become vicious. So the fact that there is *some* sort of connection between genes, neurology, and violence is well established.

Some researchers believe that this tells us something important about crime. The general notion of "crime" is too socially variable to be of much use—fornication, gambling, and heresy, for example, are sometimes counted as "crimes" and sometimes not. But suppose we focus on violent crimes—for example, murder, assault, and rape. Is it "in the genes" for some people, but not others, to do violence? The evidence suggests so.

Darrow believed that Leopold and Loeb were "born bad" because they were born without such feelings as pity and sympathy. There is no way for us to know the precise truth about Leopold and Loeb, but on the more general issue Darrow might have been right. The psychologist Judith Rich Harris (1938–) puts it like this:

> Though we no longer say that some children are born bad, the facts are such, unfortunately, that a euphemism is needed. Now psychologists say that some children are born with "difficult" temperaments—difficult for their parents to rear, difficult to socialize. I can list for you some of the things that make a child difficult to rear and difficult to socialize: a tendency to be active, impulsive, aggressive, and quick to anger; a tendency to get bored with routine activities and to seek excitement; a tendency to be unafraid of getting hurt; an insensitivity to the feelings of others; and, more often than not, a muscular build and an IQ a little lower than average. All of these characteristics have a significant genetic component.

It is easy to understand why such ideas arouse controversy. It sounds like we are being told that some children are beyond help—they're born bad, and bad they'll stay. But the fact that genes contribute to some undesirable traits does not imply that the children who have them are lost causes. For one thing, researchers now believe that there are "orchid children" who have the genetic tendency to "wilt if ignored or maltreated but bloom spectacularly with greenhouse care." If such children appear to be beyond help, this is only because they haven't yet been placed in the right environment. Moreover, no social scientist believes that genes determine everything. Your genes might incline you, in certain environments, to act in certain ways, but whether you actually behave in those ways will depend on other things. Thus, education and the elimination of poverty are still important. The research about genes only explains why virtue comes easier to some than to others.

But even if ill-behaved children might improve, we are being told something disturbing: Human beings come equipped by nature with deep-seated desires that we can resist only with difficulty. If, in some people, these desires prove irresistible, it is hard to see this as their fault. Moreover, these desires might be with us forever, and they play a significant role in our behavior. This may not be Determinism, but it sounds suspiciously close to it.

Conclusion. The case against free will comes from several parts of science. In general, scientists assume that the universe is governed by the laws of nature—by the laws of physics, chemistry, and biology. So far, everything we know about the human brain suggests that it is no exception: neurological events, including the events that cause us to act, appear to be governed by the same natural laws that govern everything else. Meanwhile, psychologists have developed a number of ideas that help explain human action. We don't know how to combine these ideas into a single, comprehensive theory of human nature, but the overall trend is not encouraging to believers in free will. Each new discovery chips away a bit more of our confidence. The more we learn about the sources of human conduct, the less room there seems to be for free choice.

CHAPTER **9**

The Debate over Free Will

Man's life is a line that nature commands him to describe on the surface of the earth, without his being able to swerve from it, even for an instant. . . . Nevertheless, in spite of the shackles by which he is bound, it is pretended he is a free agent.

—PAUL HENRI BARON D'HOLBACH,
THE SYSTEM OF NATURE (1770)

Sir, we *know* our will is free, and *there's* an end on it.

—DR. JOHNSON, IN BOSWELL'S
THE LIFE OF SAMUEL JOHNSON, LL.D. (1791)

9.1. The Determinist Argument

When asked about his philosophy of life, the novelist Isaac Bashevis Singer (1904–1991) liked to tell his friends: "I believe in free will. I have no choice." Singer's little joke makes a serious point: It is hard to avoid thinking that you have free will. When you are deciding what to do, the choice seems entirely yours. The inner feeling of freedom is so powerful that we may be unable to give up the idea of free will, no matter how much evidence there is against it.

And there is a lot of evidence against it. The more we learn about the causes of human behavior, the less likely it seems that we're free. No one piece of evidence forces this conclusion. Nonetheless, many different strands of evidence point in this direction, and the cumulative effect is that "free will" looks more and more like part of a prescientific way of thinking.

According to Determinism, everything that happens must happen, given the Laws of Nature and the past history of the universe. We may call this the Determinist Argument:

(1) Everything we do is caused by forces over which we have no control.

(2) If our actions are caused by forces over which we have no control, we do not act freely.

(3) Therefore, we never act freely.

This is a disturbing line of thought because of what it seems to imply about individual responsibility. If we are not free, then it seems that we are not responsible for what we do.

Why should we accept the first premise—why should we believe that our actions are caused by forces outside of our control? The main reason is that we are part of nature. Our bodies and our brains are composed of atoms, and like everything else composed of atoms, they are subject to the laws of physics. And we, of course, have no control over the laws of physics—these laws existed before we were born, and they will continue to operate after we die. Therefore, human actions are just like other natural events—they are due to the Laws of Nature and to prior circumstances over which we have no control.

Is the Determinist Argument sound? It is plausible, but it can be disputed. We will look at two responses to the argument. One theory, Libertarianism, denies the first premise of the argument and holds that our actions are not determined by forces beyond our control. Another theory, Compatibilism, denies the second premise and holds that we can be free *even if* our actions are determined by outside forces.

9.2. The Libertarian Response

Libertarianism is the view that at least some of our actions are not forced on us by the Laws of Nature. Rather, we freely choose to perform those actions, and nothing makes us do so. We could act differently, but we choose not to. According to this theory, human choices are not constrained like other events are. A billiard ball, when struck by another billiard ball, must move in a certain direction with a certain velocity. It has no choice; the laws of physics determine precisely what will happen. But right now, you can decide whether to continue reading or to stop reading. You can do either, and nothing makes you choose one way or the other. The Laws of Nature do not control you.

Several arguments have been given in favor of this theory.

The Argument from Experience. We may begin with the idea that we know we are free because *each of us is immediately aware of being free* every time we make a conscious choice. Think again of what you are doing at this moment. You can continue reading, or you can stop. Which will it be? Think of what it is like, right now, as you consider these options. You feel no constraints. Nothing is holding you back or forcing you in either direction. The decision is up to you. The experience of freedom, it may be said, is the best proof we could have on the matter. As Samuel Johnson told his friend Boswell, "You are surer that you can lift up your finger or not as you please, than you are of any conclusion from a deduction of reasoning."

The problem is that the evidence against free will undermines our confidence in our experience. The scientist Jose Delgado found that he could cause people to do things by electrically stimulating their brains—he could get them to look over their shoulder, for example—and then they would offer reasons why they had done so. They would say things like, "I was looking for my comb." Delgado's subjects, who did not know their brains were being stimulated, would *experience* the movements as free and voluntary. Perhaps we are like Delgado's subjects. What is the difference between us and them, except that in the experimental setting we know about the electrochemical events that cause the action, while in everyday life we don't know what's happening in our brains? In the face of such evidence, it is hollow to insist, with Dr. Johnson, that we simply know we are free. If freedom is to be defended, a better argument is needed.

The Argument That the Universe Is Not a Deterministic System. Determinism goes against present-day science. In the heyday of Newtonian physics, the universe was believed to operate according to strict laws of cause and effect. The Laws of Nature were believed to specify the conditions under which one state of affairs *must* follow another—the motion of balls on a pool table was a model for the whole universe. But in the twentieth century, Newtonian physics was replaced by a theory called quantum mechanics, which implied a different view of nature.

According to quantum mechanics, the laws that govern the behavior of matter are probabilistic. The laws do not say, "Given X, Y *must* follow." Instead, they say, "Given X, there is *a specific probability* that Y will follow." For example, suppose that a radioactive substance is decaying. The Laws of Nature may tell us that a certain percentage of the atoms are likely to decay in the next month. However, the laws will not tell us exactly which atoms will decay. That's left undetermined.

Some scientists believe, on philosophical grounds, that quantum mechanics cannot be right. "God does not play dice with the universe," said Albert Einstein (1879–1955). Einstein believed that quantum mechanics was incomplete. Eventually, he thought, we would learn more, and our new theory would be deterministic. So far, however, Einstein's prediction has proved wrong. Quantum mechanics, with its built-in uncertainties, remains one of the most powerful and successful theories in the history of science.

Does this mean that we needn't worry about Determinism? Quantum mechanics has sometimes been hailed as good news for free will. If some things are not determined by the Laws of Nature, it is said, then we might be free, because our actions might be among those undetermined things.

However, quantum physics does not offer much help in defending free will, for two reasons. First, quantum mechanics interprets nature as containing a lot of randomness—it is random and unpredictable which radioactive atoms will decay. However, these random events occur everywhere in nature, not just in human bodies. Is free will supposed to pervade every bit of matter, in every corner of the universe? No, because freedom is not the same thing as randomness. Second, the implications of quantum indeterminacy for human behavior are probably very small. Consider the implications of quantum mechanics for computers. A computer's outputs are determined by its inputs and its program. Quantum mechanics does not imply that we should stop trusting computers. According to quantum theory, a computer might randomly deviate from its program, but the chances of this happening are very, very small. The computer's operations are, if not completely determined, then close enough as to make no difference. We will almost always get the expected outputs, given the right program and the right inputs. Something similar could be true of human beings. If so, that would be enough for the Determinist Argument.

The Argument That We Cannot Predict Our Own Decisions. A different argument for Libertarianism exploits the idea that anything which is causally determined is predictable. The tree outside my window is leaning, and sooner or later it will fall. If I knew all the Laws of Nature, and if I knew everything about the tree and its physical environment, I could predict exactly when it will fall. Of course, I don't know those things, so I can't make that prediction. We might say that causally determined events are predictable *in principle,* if not always in practice.

If human actions are determined by forces outside our control, then they too should be predictable in principle. We would only need to know the pertinent facts about the person, the person's circumstances, and the relevant Laws of Nature. However, you could not always predict your own actions, even in principle. For example, suppose you were trying to decide between going out for pizza with your friends and staying home and having leftovers. Could you, in principle, predict what you'll do? Even if you knew everything about your brain, you couldn't do it. The problem is that, once you made the prediction, you could change your mind, just to keep things interesting. If you predict that you'll go out with your friends, then you could decide to stay home, just to prove a point about free will. This seems to show that there is a big difference between human actions and other events.

We may summarize the argument like this:

(1) If human actions are determined by forces beyond our control, then they are in principle predictable.

(2) But a prediction about human action can be thwarted if the person knows about the prediction and chooses to act differently.

(3) Therefore, not all human actions are in principle predictable.

(4) And so, not all human actions are determined by forces beyond our control.

This is a clever argument, but is it sound? Unfortunately, the argument fails once we examine what the word "predictable" means. There are two types of predictability:

(a) Predictable by an ideal observer who stands outside the system and observes events but does not interfere with them

(b) Predictable by you in the real world

Determinism implies predictability in sense (a) but not in sense (b). Suppose you predict you'll have pizza, and then you decide against it. Your prediction was indeed proved wrong. However, an ideal observer might have known exactly what was going to happen—she might have been able to predict your prediction as well as your decision to do the opposite. Everything might still be determined.

This argument, then, doesn't prove that our actions are up to us. But there is one more argument to consider.

The Argument from Accountability. The assumption that we have free will is deeply engrained in our ordinary ways of thinking. As we interact with other people, we cannot help but think of them as the authors of their actions. We hold them responsible, blaming them if they behave badly and admiring them if they behave well. For these attitudes to be justified, people must have free will.

Similarly, in thinking about ourselves, we assume that we have free will. Someone who hits the winning basket or aces a test may feel proud, while someone who chokes or cheats may feel ashamed. These feelings of pride and shame would be baseless if our actions were always due to factors beyond our control. Yet these feelings are inescapable. We must think of human beings as free.

We might therefore reason as follows:

(1) We cannot help but admire or blame people for what they do, nor can we avoid feeling pride or shame for what we do.

(2) These responses—admiration, blame, pride, and shame—presuppose that people have free will.

(3) Therefore, we must believe that people have free will.

(4) Since we must believe it, it is true: People have free will.

The problem with this argument is obvious: Our attitudes might be unjustified, even if they're inescapable. Step 4 is therefore unwarranted. The argument engages in a kind of wishful thinking.

Is Libertarianism Coherent? Finally, we may consider whether Libertarianism makes any sense as a positive view of human behavior. To understand our behavior, we need more than just the denial that our actions are determined by outside forces. We need, in addition, a positive account of how we make decisions.

If our actions are not determined by the Laws of Nature, how are they supposed to come about? What, exactly, produces our decisions? We might imagine that there is, inside each of us, a sort of "mental being" whose decisions are not constrained by the Laws of Nature—a ghostly controller who makes choices independently of the happenings in the brain. But this is not credible. It goes against what science tells us. There is no evidence for any sort of "mental energy" at work within us, disconnected from the operation of our neurological systems.

But if we don't say that a disconnected mental entity inside us calls the shots, what do we say? Are we supposed to think that some part of the brain operates outside the causal network of the world? It sounds silly, but it is hard to come up with anything better. There seems to be no plausible story that makes sense of Libertarian "freedom." Without such an account, we must look elsewhere for a solution to the problem of free will.

9.3. The Compatibilist Response

Compatibilism is the idea that an act can be both free and determined at the same time. This may sound like a contradiction, but according to this theory, it is not. Contrary to what you might think, we can accept the idea that human behavior is free while also acknowledging that it is determined by the Laws of Nature.

Compatibilism has always enjoyed a following in philosophy. In one form or another, it was the theory of Hobbes, Hume, Kant, and Mill, and it is defended by many writers today. This usually comes as a surprise to people who are not familiar with the philosophical literature, because free will and Determinism seem obviously *in*compatible. How are they supposed to go together? How can an act be free and determined at the same time?

According to Compatibilism, some actions are obviously free, and some are obviously not free. The trick is to see the difference between them. Here are some examples of when your action is not free:

- You hand over your wallet because a robber points his gun at you.
- You attend the company picnic because your boss tells you to.
- You report for induction into the army because you've been drafted.

In these cases, you are not acting freely because you are being forced to do things you don't want to do. On the other hand, here are some cases in which you do act freely:

- You contribute money to a charity because you believe that the charity deserves your support.
- You urge your company to sponsor a picnic because you think it would be fun. You're delighted when your boss agrees, and you volunteer to organize the event.
- You join the army because you want to fight the enemy.

These actions are free because your choice is based on your own desires, without anyone else telling you what to do. *This is what it means to do something "of your own free will."* But notice that this is perfectly compatible with your actions being causally determined by your past history, by events in your brain, and so on. It is even compatible with your *desires* being caused by factors beyond your control. The theory says that, to act freely, you must act according to your desires. However, the theory says nothing about where those desires came from. Thus, free will and Determinism are compatible.

According to Compatibilism, a free action might be predictable. Is that a problem for the theory? Consider an example. I have a friend who sees lots of movies, and I know what sorts of movies she likes. I have been observing her moviegoing habits for years. If she is picking a movie to watch tonight, and I know the options, I can almost always predict what she will choose. Does this mean she isn't free? Not at all—she looks at what's playing, thinks over what she wants to see, and decides accordingly. No one is threatening her. No one is manipulating her or tricking her. No one has planted a remote-control device in her brain. Thus, she chooses "of her own free will." The fact that I can predict her choice changes nothing. Indeed, something would be wrong if I could *not* predict that she will prefer *The Blind Side* to *No Country for Old Men.*

The basic idea of Compatibilism may be summed up like this: Free will is compatible with causal determinism because "free" does not mean "uncaused." Rather, it means something like "uncoerced." You are free when you act according to your own wishes and desires.

Free Will as Involving Determinism. The main argument for Compatibilism goes as follows. The whole worry over free will begins with the idea that *if an action is part of the great causal chain, it cannot be free.* In other words, if human actions are like other events, subject to prior causes and controlled by the laws of physics, then we are no more free than a feather tossed about by the wind. The question, then, is whether this idea is true.

If no *caused* action could be free, then what could free actions be like? Presumably, they would have to be uncaused—they would have to be outside the great causal chain. But consider what that would mean. What would it be like for *any* event to be uncaused? Imagine that billiard balls stopped obeying the laws of physics. Their motions would then be unpredictable, but only because they would be random and chaotic. The balls might go off at odd angles, leap into the air, or suddenly stop. When struck by the cue ball, the eight ball might not move at all. Or it might explode, or turn to ice. Anything could happen.

Similarly, if a person's actions were suddenly disconnected from the network of causes and effects, they would become random, chaotic, and unpredictable. A man standing on a street corner might step into traffic rather than wait for the light to change. He might attack the dog next to him as he recites the Magna Carta. This is what it might be like for behavior to be uncaused. But it is not what we mean by "free." You would not think that someone who behaved in this way had free will—you would think that he was crazy. Free actions are not random and chaotic.

According to Compatibilism, freedom is not only compatible with Determinism; freedom *requires* Determinism, at least in the realm of human action. In a random, chaotic world, no one would be free, because free actions must be orderly and thoughtful. But in a world that operates according to the Laws of Nature, free action is possible. In such a world, a person's character and desires can control what he does.

The Problem with Compatibilism. Compatibilism is a successful theory, in that it makes sense of how people actually talk: we do indeed say that people act "of their own free will" when they act according to their own wishes and values. However, historically, the debate about free will has been about something deeper than how people talk: it has been about the nature of human action and its relationship to moral responsibility. Peter van Inwagen (1942–) makes the deep case against Compatibilism like this:

> If Determinism is true, then our actions are consequences of the laws of nature and events in the remote past. But it is not up to us what went on before we were born, and neither is it up to us what the laws of nature are. Therefore, the consequences of these things (including our present acts) are not up to us.

The compatibilist might respond by saying that, even if Determinism is true, our actions could still be "up to us" in the sense that we could perform those actions according to our own desires and values. However, van Inwagen's argument can be extended to our desires and values themselves: If Determinism is true, then our desires and values are themselves consequences of the laws of nature and events in the remote past. But those laws and those events are not up to us. Therefore, our desires and values are not up to us. This is a point that compatibilists must concede. But that concession seems to give away the game. If my actions depend on my desires and values, and my desires and values are not up to me, then my actions seem not to be up to me, either. So, free will does not appear to be compatible with Determinism after all.

9.4. Ethics and Free Will

Many philosophers and theologians see the deterministic implications of modern science as a crisis. Our freedom, they say, is essential to our dignity as moral beings. It separates us from the animals. If we start thinking of ourselves as mere robots, pushed around by impersonal forces, we lose our humanity.

But before we give in to such fears, we need to ask what the implications of Determinism really are. If we do not have free will, are we still responsible moral agents? Does ethics lose its point?

Robots, Fatalism, and Deliberation. We can set aside the idea that if we lack free will, then we are "mere robots." We are nothing like robots. We have thoughts, intentions, and emotions. We experience happiness and unhappiness. We love our children and, if we are lucky, they love us back. We take pleasure in going to parties, playing Xbox, and listening to music. None of this is true of robots.

Also unlike robots, we often have *reasons* for what we do, and this will be true even if we lack free will. As long as our beliefs and desires can guide our behavior, we can act rationally. We can still pursue our own goals, just as before. Of course, the sense in which our goals are "our own" would change. We could no longer think of them as something that we freely choose. Instead, we would see them as the result of our genes, our environment, and the working of our brains. But so what? They would still be our goals, and we would still care about them.

It is sometimes suggested that the denial of free will would lead to a fatalistic attitude about the future: There would be no point in striving to change things, because the future must follow a set path. But this does not follow. The future depends on what we do, and if we want a certain sort of future, we have good reason to bring it about. Suppose you want sick children in Niger to get medical care, and so you contribute to humanitarian efforts. You help change the future. And there is certainly a point to it—without the help, the children will be worse off. The presence or absence of free will makes no difference.

Could we *deliberate* about what to do if we had no free will? Some philosophers think that, if we're not free, then "deliberating" makes no sense. After all, deliberating means trying to decide, and trying to decide seems to presuppose that we could do different things. This reasoning sounds plausible. But what do we actually do when we deliberate? Mainly, we think about what we want and about how different actions would lead to different outcomes. We think about the children in Niger, what it's like to be sick and helpless, how our money could supply their needs, and so on; and we might think about other things we could use our money for. Nothing in all that presupposes freedom.

Nor does the denial of free will mean the end of ethics. We may still regard some things as good and others as bad—even if no one has free will, it is still better for the children in Niger not to die. We may still regard actions as better or worse depending on their consequences—contributing to humanitarian efforts is a good thing, even if we lack free will. And we can still think about all this in deciding what to do.

Evaluating People as Good or Bad. Can we continue to regard *people* as good or bad if they lack free will? In a sense, we certainly can. Even without free will, people will still have virtues and vices. They will still be brave or cowardly, kind or cruel, generous or greedy. A murderer will still be a killer, and a killer will still be a bad thing to be. Of course, it may be possible to explain someone's misdeeds as the result of his genes, his history, or the chemistry of his brain. And this may lead us to view him as unlucky. But that doesn't mean he is not bad. We need to distinguish *whether* someone is bad from *how he came to be* bad. A causal account of someone's character doesn't imply he isn't bad. It merely explains how he got to be that way.

Consider again Eric Rudolph, whose terrorist bombing spree in the 1990s killed two people and injured over 100 others. Rudolph's life story provides ample evidence that he is not responsible for how he turned out. As one journalist put it, Rudolph was "the product of a paranoid fringe of white supremacists, religious zealots and government haters." Knowing his background, we may regard him as unlucky. As the old saying has it, there but for the grace of God go I. Yet we may still think of Rudolph as bad, because he is, after all, a murderer. He deliberately tried to harm innocent people. These things are true even if we understand what made him that way.

Responsibility. But, it may be protested, if people do not have free will, then they are not *responsible* for what they do. Philosophers disagree about whether this conclusion would be disturbing or enlightened. Bertrand Russell (1872–1970) thought it enlightened. He wrote:

> No man treats a motorcar as foolishly as he treats another human being. When the car will not go, he does not

attribute its annoying behavior to sin; he does not say, "You are a wicked motorcar, and I shall not give you any more petrol until you go." He attempts to find out what is wrong and to set it right.

Similarly, Russell says, when a person misbehaves, we should try to figure out why and deal with that.

However, it is not clear whether the conclusion is correct—perhaps we can be responsible even if we're not free. So let's see if we can develop an account of responsibility that goes along with Determinism. Being responsible means, at least, that you may be held accountable for what you do—you may be blamed when you behave badly and praised when you behave well. So, if you are a responsible being, there must be some conditions under which you deserve blame for an action. There seem to be three such conditions: (a) you must have done the act in question, (b) the act must have been wrong, and (c) you must have no excuse for having done it.

The notion of an excuse is crucial. Excuses are facts that get you off the hook when you have done something bad. It was an accident, you may say, or you didn't know what you were doing, or you were forced to do it. Here are some common excuses:

- *Mistake.* When you left my apartment, you took my umbrella by mistake—you thought it was yours. If you had taken my umbrella intentionally, you would deserve blame.
- *Accident.* You were driving safely, taking every precaution, when a child darted in front of the car, and you hit her. If you had been trying to hit her, or if you had been driving carelessly, you could be blamed.
- *Coercion.* You were forced to open the company safe because the robbers threatened you. If you had opened it voluntarily, you could be blamed.
- *Ignorance.* You gave your boyfriend a deadly poison because the bottle was mislabeled. If you had known it was poison, you'd be a murderer.
- *Illness.* You mistreated your sister because you suffer from Capgras syndrome. This is a rare delusional disorder that makes people believe that someone they know has been replaced by an imposter. So, your behavior is not your fault.

The logic of praise is similar to the logic of blame. You deserve praise for an action if (a) you did it, (b) it was a good thing to do, and (c) there are no conditions present that are analogous to excuses. It is curious that we have no name for these analogous conditions. We have a word, "excuses," for the conditions that make blame inappropriate; but we have no word for the conditions that make praise inappropriate. Yet, clearly, similar ideas apply. If you do something good, but you do it merely by accident or from ignorance, then you do not deserve praise. Perhaps there is no general word for these conditions because people are usually happy to receive praise, regardless of whether they deserve it. Let's call these conditions "praise-busters."

According to this account of responsibility, people are responsible for what they do if there are no excusing conditions or praise-busters present. Then, if they behave well, they merit praise; and if they behave badly, they deserve blame. Nothing in this account conflicts with the assumption of Determinism.

Is Something Still Missing? If we lack free will, there is still a sense in which we can be good or bad. Our actions can still have good or bad consequences, and we can still talk about whether a person has any of the standard excuses for her actions. But something feels missing here. Don't we want to evaluate people in more ways than this? Without free will, we can evaluate people only as we now evaluate dogs. Some dogs are gentle and sweet; others are mean and vicious. In this vein, we speak of "good dogs" and "bad dogs." However, we normally think of human beings as capable of a higher goodness—a *moral* goodness. People, we believe, can freely create value. They can freely choose to do what's right or to do what's wrong. Dogs can't.

Next, consider the notion of responsibility. If you're training a puppy to be a good companion, you treat her as if she were responsible: you punish her for behaving badly, and you reward her for behaving well. Moreover, as part of the training, you acknowledge some excuses on her behalf (she can't be expected to resist eating meat that has been left out too temptingly), and you reject other alleged excuses (she *can* resist the urge to beg for meat at the table). However, none of us would say that dogs are "really" responsible for what they do; rather, we would say that sometimes we treat dogs *as if they were responsible*, based on the benefits of doing so, even though we know that dogs are not responsible. If human beings lack free will, shouldn't we say the same about humans—shouldn't we say that people are not really responsible for what they do, even though it is often useful to treat them as though they were? People could be "really responsible" only if they had free will.

Also, without free will, it would be odd to criticize anyone for anything he has done. After all, he had to do it. For example, suppose that a member of the president's inner circle lies at a congressional hearing. If there is no free will, then the Laws of Nature compelled him to lie—he couldn't have done otherwise. To say that he should have been truthful would be absurd; it would be like saying that he should have jumped over the moon—both actions were impossible for him at that time. To say that the official ought to have been honest would thus violate the principle, *ought implies can*. This is the principle that if you *ought* to do something, then it must be true that you *can* do it. If we lack free will, then all moral criticisms would violate this principle, because it would never be true that we "could" have done something that we didn't do.

Those who reject free will might respond in one of two ways. On the one hand, they might embrace the idea that no one can ever be rightfully blamed for their actions. This position is defensible, though it goes against common sense. On the other hand, they might interpret the ought-implies-can principle in this way: "To say that you ought to do X implies that you 'can' do X *in the sense that doing X is within your general physical power*." Not lying *is* within our general physical power, so it makes sense to say that we ought not to lie. However, jumping over the moon is not within our general physical power, so it makes no sense to say that we ought to jump over the moon. By embracing the ought-implies-can principle in this form, we ensure that we will make moral judgments only about actions that we could conceivably influence—namely, actions that are within our general physical power. For example, we could conceivably influence someone not to lie (by affecting his brain chemistry in the right way), but we could never influence someone to jump over the moon (no change in brain chemistry could make someone's legs that powerful). If we accept these assumptions, then we can still praise and blame people for their actions, and our use of the word "ought" will have a practical point, namely, to try to influence people's behavior. However, the whole business of praise and blame would sound more like manipulation—like a sophisticated form of dog training—than like the recognition of a deep moral truth about the other person's behavior.

A belief in free will, therefore, does seem necessary to retain our commonsense picture of moral agency. However, that picture might be incorrect.

CHAPTER 11

Ethics and Objectivity

There are no objective values.
—J. L. MACKIE, *ETHICS: INVENTING RIGHT AND WRONG* (1977)

11.1. Thrasymachus's Challenge

Thrasymachus has the misfortune of being remembered through the eyes of someone who despised him. He was a Sophist, one of the professional teachers who flourished in Athens during the time of Socrates (ca. 470–399 B.C.). We know about Socrates through the writings of his student Plato. Plato tells us that the Sophists, unlike Socrates, charged a fee for their instruction, and he is quick to insinuate that the Sophists liked money more than truth. Plato is especially hard on Thrasymachus, who is introduced in the *Republic* like this:

> While we had been talking [says Socrates] Thrasymachus had often tried to interrupt, but had been prevented by those sitting near him, who wanted to hear the argument concluded; but when we paused, he was no longer able to contain himself and gathered himself together and sprang on us like a wild beast, as if he wanted to tear us in pieces. Polemarchus and I were scared stiff, as Thrasymachus burst out and said, "What is all this nonsense, Socrates?"

The "nonsense" was a discussion of justice. Thrasymachus was impatient because Socrates and his friends were assuming that justice is something real and important. But according to Thrasymachus, people believe in right and wrong only because they are taught to obey the rules of their society. Those rules, however, are merely human inventions. Thrasymachus added that the rules of a society will protect the interests of the society's

139

most powerful members. So, when ordinary people think they must "do the right thing," they are just being played.

Throughout history, there have always been groups of people who, like Thrasymachus, believe that ethics is just a matter of opinion; and there have always been groups of people who, like Socrates, believe that ethics has an objective basis. But with the rise of modern science, skepticism about ethics became even more attractive. Modern science sees the world as a cold, indifferent place that cares nothing for us or our projects; the universe is a realm of facts that know nothing of right or wrong. As David Hume (1711–1776) put it, "The life of a man is of no greater importance to the universe than that of an oyster." Thus, it seems natural to conclude that ethics can be nothing but a human creation.

Thrasymachus challenged Socrates to prove that ethics has an objective basis. One way of meeting Thrasymachus's challenge might be to introduce religious notions. If the universe was created by God, according to a divine plan, and if God issues commands about how we should live, we might find in this an objective basis for our judgments of right and wrong. But suppose we set this possibility aside. Is there any way to defend the objectivity of ethics without invoking religion? We will see that there is a way. The arguments for ethical skepticism are not as powerful as they appear.

11.2. Is Ethics Just a Matter of Social Conventions?

The idea that ethics is nothing more than social convention has always appealed to educated people. Different cultures have different moral codes, it is said, and it is merely naïve to think that there is one universal standard that applies in all places and times. Examples of differences are easy to come by. In Islamic countries, men may have more than one wife. In medieval Europe, lending money for interest was considered a sin. In northern Greenland, old people were sometimes left to die in the snow. Considering such examples, anthropologists have long agreed with Herodotus, the ancient historian who said, "Custom is king o'er all."

Today, the idea of morality as a social product is attractive for an additional reason. Given America's economic power and military might, it is especially important for Americans to respect and appreciate the differences between cultures. In particular, it is said, we must avoid the arrogant assumption that our ways are "right" and that other ways are "wrong." This means, in part, that we should refrain from making moral judgments about other cultures. We should adopt a policy of live and let live.

On the surface, this attitude seems enlightened. Tolerance is important, and many cultural practices are nothing more than social customs—standards of dress, the details of household arrangements, the methods of greeting, and so on. But fundamental matters of justice are different. When we consider such examples as slavery, racism, and the abuse of women, it no longer seems enlightened to shrug and say, "They have their customs, and we have ours." Consider two examples.

In a Pakistani village, a 12-year-old boy was accused of being romantically involved with a 22-year-old woman of a higher social class. He denied it, but the tribal elders did not believe him. As punishment, they decreed that the boy's teenage sister— who had done nothing wrong—should be publicly raped. Her name is Mukhtar Mai. Four men carried out the sentence while the village watched. Observers said there was nothing unusual in this, but with so many foreigners in the region, the incident was noticed and reported in *Newsweek*. This was in 2002.

In the same year, in northern Nigeria, a religious court sentenced an unwed mother named Amina Lawal to be stoned to death for having had sex out of wedlock. When the verdict was read, the crowd in the courtroom cheered, and the judge said that the sentence should be carried out as soon as Lawal's baby was old enough not to need breast-feeding. Lawal identified the father, but he denied the accusation, and no charges were brought against him. This was only one in a series of such sentences imposed in northern Nigeria. Responding to international pressure, the Nigerian government announced that it would not enforce the sentence against Lawal, and in 2004 she was set free.

The rape of Mukhtar Mai was regarded as a matter of tribal honor. Her brother was allegedly romancing a woman from a different tribe, and the elders of her tribe demanded justice. The stonings in Nigeria, on the other hand, are the application of the Islamic law of Sharia, which has been adopted by 12 of Nigeria's 36 states. Our instincts are to condemn both punishments. But are we *justified* in condemning them? Two thoughts stand in the way of saying we are.

First, there is the idea that *we should respect the differences between cultures.* People in other cultures have a right to follow their own traditions, it is said, even if outsiders like us disapprove. After all, their traditions may have a purpose that we don't understand. Moreover, it is said, their values might be different from ours. Should thoughts like these persuade us to hold our tongues when we hear about a raping or a stoning on the other side of the world?

They should not. Respecting a culture does not mean tolerating everything in it. You might think that a culture has a wonderful history and has produced great art. You might think that its leading figures are admirable and that your own culture has much to learn from them. Yet, despite all this, you need not regard the culture as perfect. You might think it contains elements that are awful. Most of us take just this attitude toward our own society—if you are an American, you probably think that America is a great country but that some aspects of our culture are appalling. Why should you not think the same about Pakistan or Nigeria? If you did, you would be agreeing with many Pakistanis and Nigerians.

Moreover, it is a mistake to think of the world as a collection of discrete, unified cultures that exist in isolation from one another. Cultures overlap and interact. In the United States, there are cultural differences between Irish Catholics, Italian Americans, Southern Baptists, African Americans in Los Angeles, African Americans in Mississippi, and Hasidic Jews in Brooklyn. Coal miners in West Virginia are quite different, culturally, from stockbrokers in New York City. In some ways we think that "live and let live" is the best policy, but no one takes this to mean that you should have no opinion about what happens in another part of the country.

This also raises the question of who speaks for a culture. Is it the priests? The politicians? The women? The slaves? Opinions within a society are rarely uniform. If we say, for example, that slavery was approved of in ancient Greece, we are referring to the opinions of the slave-owners. The slaves themselves might have had a different opinion. Or consider again the public raping of Mukhtar Mai. When this happened, the Pakistani government took action against the tribal leaders who had ordered it. Which group—the local leaders or the national government—sets the standards that we must respect? There are no clear-cut answers to these questions. Thus, it is often unhelpful to say, "We must respect the values of the culture."

Finally, we should notice a purely logical point. Some people think that ethical relativism *follows from* the fact that cultures have different standards. That is, they endorse this argument:

(1) Different cultures have different moral codes.

(2) Therefore, there is no such thing as objective right and wrong. Where ethics is concerned, the standards of the different societies are all that exist.

But this is a mistake. It does not follow from the fact that people disagree about something, that there is no truth about it. For example, cultures may disagree about the Milky Way—some think it's a galaxy, others think it's a river in the sky—but it does not follow from this that there is no objective truth about the Milky Way. The same goes for ethics. When cultures employ different customs, some of the customs may be better than others. It is easy to overlook this if we only think of trivial examples, such as the standards of dress at a wedding or funeral. Those may indeed be nothing but matters of local custom. But it does not follow that *all* practices are merely matters of local custom. Fundamental matters of justice might be different.

Thus, we needn't refrain from morally assessing the customs of other societies. We can be tolerant and respectful, yet think that other cultures are flawed.

There is, however, a second reason why being judgmental may seem inappropriate: all standards may seem to be culture-relative. If we say that the rape of Mukhtar Mai was wrong, we are using *our* standards to judge *their* practices. From our point of view, the rape was wrong, but why is our point of view correct? We can say that the tribal leaders are wrong, but they can equally well say that we are wrong. How can we get beyond this mutual finger-pointing?

This second argument can be spelled out as follows:

(1) For our criticisms of other cultures to be justified, they must appeal to standards that are not simply derived from our own culture.

(2) But there are no such culture-neutral moral standards. All standards are relative to some society or other.

(3) Therefore, our criticisms of other cultures are unjustified.

Is this correct? It sounds plausible, but in fact there *is* a culture-neutral standard of right and wrong. The reason we object to the rape and the stoning is not that they are "contrary to American values." Nor is our objection that these practices are somehow bad for *us*. We object because of the harm done to Mukhtar Mai and Amina Lawal. Our culture-neutral standard is *whether the social practice in question is beneficial or harmful to the people who are affected by it.* Good social practices benefit people; bad social practices harm people.

This standard is culture-neutral in every relevant sense. First, it does not play favorites between cultures. It may be applied equally to all societies, including our own. Second, the source of the principle does not lie within one particular culture. Rather, every culture values the welfare of its people. It is a value that must be embraced, at least to some extent, by every culture, if the culture is to exist. And so, the suggestion that a social practice is harmful can never be dismissed as an alien standard "brought in from the outside."

11.3. Ethics and Science

We think of science as the most objective human enterprise. Scientists know how to get at the truth. The study of ethics, however, seems unlike science. So how can ethics be objective? Let's consider three arguments along these lines.

The Argument from Disagreement. It is troubling that ethical disagreement seems so widespread and persistent. If ethics were a matter of objective truth, shouldn't we expect more consensus? Yet it seems that, in matters of ethics, people disagree about everything. They argue over abortion, capital punishment, gun control, euthanasia, the environment, and the moral status of animals. They disagree about sex, drug use, and whether we have a duty to help needy children in foreign countries. In science, however, there is widespread agreement on all essential points. The natural conclusion is that ethics, unlike science, is a mere matter of opinion. We may summarize the argument like this:

> **(1)** In ethics, unlike in science, there is widespread and persistent disagreement.

(2) The best explanation of this fact is that there is no objective truth in ethics.

(3) Therefore, we may conclude, at least tentatively, that there is no objective truth in ethics.

Is this argument sound? We may begin by observing that ethics is more like science than people think. There is a tremendous amount of agreement in ethics. All thoughtful people agree that murder, rape, theft, child abuse, blackmail, kidnapping, and racism are wrong. Everyone agrees that we should tell the truth, help our friends, keep our promises, and love our children. If it is said that some people do not agree—racists and thieves, for example—it can be replied that some people disagree with the findings of science—flat-earthers and psychics, for example. The situation in ethics is the same as in science: The vast majority of people agree, while some dissenters are ignored, for good reason. In fact, there may be more dissenters in science than in ethics, if you count religious fundamentalists who reject Darwin's theory of evolution.

In ethics, then, there is massive agreement about simple matters. But there is also disagreement about abortion, capital punishment, and the other issues mentioned above. What should we make of this? We might notice, first, that from a social point of view, most of the matters we disagree on are less important than the matters we agree on. No matter how much people care about gun control, for example, gun control is less important than murder, truth telling, or promise keeping. After all, societies can function with a variety of policies on guns. But social living would be impossible without a rule against murder. Likewise, society would be impossible if people could lie and break their promises at will. To see this, try to imagine what it would be like to live in a place where people could lie, cheat, steal, and kill with impunity. That society would collapse.

We might also notice that many of the disputed issues are *harder* than the matters we agree on. In order to take a principled stand on abortion, for example, we would have to figure out whether the fetus's life is precious. Thus, we would have to answer the question: When, in the course of human development, does human life acquire its full value? Moreover, we might have to assess the importance of potentiality: Does the fact that the fetus *might one day* become a full human person affect the fetus's moral status *today*? All this is hard enough, but to make things worse, it is not obvious that these are even the right questions to ask. We could instead ask about the rights of the pregnant woman, or about how large the human population should be. So, it is no wonder that people disagree about the morality of abortion. In such cases, the difficulty of the issues, and not the absence of "truth," is the best explanation of why people don't agree.

A similar pattern of agreement and disagreement exists in science. All scientists agree about a large central core of accepted truth. Yet many others issues are disputed. Scientists disagree about the path that evolution has taken, the prospects for string theory, what is really shown by the groundbreaking experiments on infant cognition, and the relation between quantum theory and classical relativity. So, contrary to superficial impressions, there does not appear to be any fundamental difference between ethics and science. Both are characterized by broad agreement alongside some disagreement.

The Argument from Lack of Proof. While scientists may disagree about some things, they agree about how to resolve their disputes. They make observations and perform experiments in order to prove or disprove their hypotheses. This means that, in science, disagreement is only temporary. But in ethics, disagreement is endless, because no one knows how to prove or disprove anything.

This argument may be summarized as follows:

(1) If there were objective truth in ethics, then it should be possible to prove that at least some ethical opinions are true.

(2) But it is not possible to prove that any ethical opinion is true.

(3) Therefore, there is no objective truth in ethics.

Is this correct? It certainly sounds plausible. Anyone who has tried to persuade someone else on an ethical matter will know how frustrating it can be. A pacifist, for example, will not be persuaded that violence is sometimes necessary, no matter what reasons are offered. Nor will a defender of violence be persuaded to change his mind, no matter how often he is told that violence only begets more violence.

If we turn to simpler examples, however, things look very different. Suppose the issue is whether a certain doctor is unethical. I say that Dr. Jones behaves shamefully, and you are surprised to hear it because you think she's a fine doctor. So I point out several things:

- Dr. Jones owns stock in a drug company, and she always prescribes that company's drugs, whether her patients need them or not.
- She won't listen to the advice of other physicians, and she becomes angry when her patients want a second opinion.
- She doesn't keep up with current medical knowledge.
- She often performs surgery while she's drunk.

Suppose all this is true. Isn't this good evidence that she is unethical? Doesn't this *prove* that she is unethical? Suppose, further, that little could be said on the other side, in her defense. Doesn't this settle the matter? What more in the way of proof could anyone want?

Other examples come easily to mind. The proof that Mr. Smith is a bad man is that he is a habitual liar who is sometimes cruel. The proof that Mr. Brown is an unethical poker player is that he cheats. The proof that Professor Adams should not have given the midterm on Tuesday is that she announced it would be given on Thursday. In each case, of course, further facts may need to be considered. But the point is that such judgments are not merely "subjective."

Ethical proofs may be different, in some ways, from scientific proofs. But that does not mean that ethical proofs are deficient. Ethical proofs consist in giving reasons to support moral conclusions. If the reasons are powerful, and if there are no good opposing considerations, then the case is made.

This may seem too quick. If ethical judgments can so obviously be proven, then why was the contrary idea so plausible in the first place? Why is it so intuitively appealing to think that there are no ethical proofs? There are at least three reasons.

First, when we think about ethics, we don't usually think about the simple matters. The fact that they are simple makes them boring, so we tend to ignore them. We are attracted instead to the harder issues, such as pacifism, abortion, and gun control. But this is what leads us astray. If we think only about the hard issues, we may naturally conclude that there are no proofs in ethics, because no one has a knockdown argument against abortion or in favor of pacifism. We might overlook the fact that proofs are easily available on the more mundane issues.

Second, there are often good reasons on both sides of a moral issue, and this leads people to despair about reaching definite conclusions. If I say that Smith is a bad man because he often lies, you may reply that Smith sometimes works for good causes. The first fact counts against him, but the second is in his favor. This feature of moral reasoning, however, should not worry us. Moral reasoning requires taking all the facts into account and weighing them against one another. Where Smith is concerned, the right conclusion might be that he is on the whole bad, even though he has some good qualities. Or the right conclusion might be that Smith is equally good and bad. It just depends on the facts. The difficult issues are like this; there is much to be said on each side.

That simple truth is often overlooked. It is common for people on one side of a debate to deny that the other side has made any good points at all. To win the debate, they feel that they must concede nothing. This, of course, means that the debate will go on endlessly. But moral debates needn't be like that. You can acknowledge that your opponent has made good, relevant points, while maintaining that your points are even better.

Finally, it is easy to confuse *proving an opinion to be true* and *persuading someone to accept your proof.* The first is a matter of sound reasoning; the second is a matter of psychology. Someone might reject a perfectly good argument because he is stubborn, or prejudiced, or simply uninterested in finding the truth. It does not follow that the argument itself is defective. A Klansman or a neo-Nazi may not listen to a sound argument about racism, but that says something about *them,* not about the argument. And there is a more general reason why people might resist listening. Accepting a moral argument often means acknowledging that we should change our behavior. And we may not want to do that. Thus, people sometimes turn a deaf ear.

The Metaphysical Argument. There is one further argument to consider, namely, that ethics cannot be objective because "values" do not exist as part of the objective world.

If we take an inventory of the world, noting all the things that exist, we can make a very long list, mentioning rocks, rivers, mountains, plants, and animals. We would find buildings, deserts, caves, iron, and oxygen. Looking up, we would see stars, comets, clouds, and galaxies. Of course, we could never complete such a list. Life is too short, there are too many things, and we are too ignorant. But we think we know, at least roughly, the *kinds* of things that exist. There are physical objects, made of atoms, that obey the laws of physics, chemistry, and biology; and there are conscious beings, such as ourselves, which may or may not be just another type of physical object.

But where, among all these things, are values? The answer, it seems, is *nowhere*. Values do not exist, at least not in the same way that rocks and rivers exist. Apart from human feelings and human interests, the world appears to contain no values. David Hume put it this way:

> Take any action allow'd to be vicious: Willful murder, for instance. Examine it in all lights, and see if you can find that matter of fact, or real existence, which you call *vice*. In whichever way you take it, you find only certain passions, motives, volitions and thoughts. There is no other matter of fact in the case. The vice entirely escapes you, as long as you consider the object. You never can find it, till you turn your reflection into your own breast, and find a sentiment of [disapproval], which arises in you, towards this action. Here is a matter of fact; but 'tis the object of feeling, not of reason.

Of course, there may be other conscious beings who also have feelings and interests—nonhuman animals, for example, and possibly the inhabitants of other planets. But they will be in the same position that we are in. They will find no values in the world around them. Only their "passions, motives, volitions, and thoughts" will give rise to values for them.

Other philosophers have taken up this theme. Friedrich Nietzsche (1844–1900) was a troubled figure who had no real home for much of his life. He moved around Europe, writing book after book, but his books were largely ignored. Eleven years before his death, he went insane. After he died, his fame grew, but he was embraced by the Nazis, who wrongly took him to support their racist causes. Later he was rescued from this misunderstanding, and today Nietzsche is seen as an original and important thinker.

Like Hume, Nietzsche denied that there are moral facts. "There are no moral phenomena at all," he wrote, "but only moral interpretations of phenomena." The right way to think about ethics, he thought, is not to focus on *morality,* as though it were one unified thing, but to study *moralities,* the historically contingent systems of value that have been created by different people at different times. Nietzsche himself wrote about a morality that underlies much of Western culture, which he called "slave morality." Slave morality, Nietzsche said, glorifies meekness, self-denial, obedience, and poverty. This outlook, he said, is unworthy of noble men, and he advocated replacing it with an ethic that emphasizes strength and dominance.

This is the "Metaphysical Argument": *Ethical opinions cannot be objectively true or false because there is no moral reality that they may match or fail to match.* This is the deep way in which ethics differs from science. Science describes a reality that exists independent of observers. If conscious beings ceased to exist, the world would otherwise be unchanged—it would still be there, and it would still be just as science describes it. But if there were no conscious beings, there would be no moral dimension to reality at all.

We may summarize the argument like this:

(1) There are objective truths in science because there is an objective reality—the physical world—which science describes.

(2) But there is no moral reality comparable to the reality of the physical world. There is nothing "there" for ethics to describe.

(3) Therefore, there are no objective truths in ethics.

Is this argument sound? It is true, I think, that there is no moral reality comparable to the reality of the physical world. However, it does not follow from this that ethics has no objective basis. After all, an inquiry might be objective in two ways:

1. It may be objective because there is an independent reality that it describes correctly or incorrectly. Science is objective in this sense.

2. An inquiry may be objective because there are reliable methods of reasoning that determine truth and falsity in its domain. Mathematics is objective in this sense. Mathematical results are objective because they are provable by the relevant kinds of arguments.

Ethics is objective in the second sense. We do not discover whether an ethical opinion is true by comparing it to some sort of "moral reality." Instead, we discover what is right by examining the reasons, or arguments, that can be given on both sides of an issue—the right thing to do is whatever there are the best reasons for doing. For ethics to be objective, it is enough that we can identify and evaluate reasons for and against ethical judgments.

11.4. The Importance of Human Interests

The preceding discussion should have dispelled most of your doubts about the objectivity of ethics. But some nagging doubts might remain, for good reason. We have not yet gotten to the bottom of things.

Every inquiry, whether in science, mathematics, or ethics, involves reasoning: We gather data, marshal arguments, and draw conclusions. But reasoning cannot go on forever. If I tell you that A is true, and you want to know why, I may cite B as my reason. If you call B into question, I may justify B by appealing to C. And so on. But at some point we come to the end of the line. Every chain of reasoning must end somewhere. This means that every argument ultimately appeals to some consideration that is simply taken for granted.

Scientific reasoning terminates when we reach simple facts about the physical world. We know, for example, that the galaxies are moving apart. How do we know this? Because of facts about the light that reaches the earth—in particular, facts about the red shift in the spectrum. How do we know what the red shift means? Because of many past observations and experiments. This example is simplified, but when we reach the simplest observed facts, we have reached the bedrock on which everything else rests. Mathematical reasoning is somewhat different in that it does not appeal to facts about the physical world. Instead, it relies on axioms, which may be taken as self-evidently true or may simply be assumed for the purposes of the proof.

Where do ethical arguments terminate? To what do they ultimately appeal? Let us look more closely at one of our previous examples. Smith is a bad man because, among other things, he is a habitual liar. This is a good reason for judging him to be morally deficient, we said, and so this fact forms part of a "proof" that he behaves unethically. But why is it bad to lie?

Lying is bad for several reasons. First, it is harmful to people. If I lie to you, and you believe me, then things can go badly for you. Suppose you ask me when the concert starts, and I say "Ten," even though I know it begins at 7:30. You arrive at 9:40 only to find that you've missed half the show. Multiply this example many times over, and you will see why honesty is important. Second, lying is a violation of trust. When you believe me without checking on what I say, you are trusting me. So, if I lie to you, I am causing you harm in a special way, by taking advantage of your trust. This is why people feel so personally affronted when they're lied to. Finally, the rule against lying is a fundamental social rule, in the sense that no society could exist without it. If we cannot assume that people will speak truthfully, then communication cannot take place; and without communication, society cannot exist.

Thus, the judgment that lying is wrong is not arbitrary. It has good reasons behind it. Suppose, though, you pushed further and wanted to know why it matters if people are harmed, or trust is violated, or society collapses. We could say a little more. We could point out that people are *worse off* when they base their decisions on false information and their trust is violated. We could point out that everyone would be worse off if people couldn't live together in cooperative societies. But you persist: Why does it matter if people are worse off? Here we come to the end of the line. Ethical reasoning terminates in considerations about people being better or worse off—or, perhaps, in considerations about *any* sensitive creature being better or worse off—just as scientific reasoning terminates in simple observations about the physical world.

Some people conclude from this that ethics is subjective—after all, ethics is ultimately about the well-being of individuals, which is a subjective matter. Personally, I don't think this is a good use of the word "subjective," but what's important is not what words we use, but what conclusions we draw from them. If ethics is subjective in the sense of being about individuals, it does not follow that ethics is arbitrary. Nor does it follow that people are free to accept whatever ethical judgments they like, or that one person's opinions will always be as good as another's. Ethics remains a matter of following reason, and it will still be objectively true that some things are good for people, and other things are bad for people. Ethical judgments can still be correct or incorrect. In these ways, the objectivity of ethics is secure.

CHAPTER 12

Why Should We Be Moral?

Immorality is the morality of those who are having a better time.
—H. L. MENCKEN,
A MENCKEN CHRESTOMATHY (1956)

12.1. The Ring of Gyges

An ancient legend tells the story of Gyges, a poor shepherd who found a magic ring in a fissure opened by an earthquake. Gyges discovered that when he twisted the ring on his finger, he would become invisible. With this great power, Gyges could go anywhere and do anything he wanted, without fear of detection. He used the ring to enrich himself, taking what he wanted and killing anyone who got in his way. Eventually, he invaded the royal palace, where he seduced the queen, murdered the king, and seized the throne.

Glaucon tells this story in Book I of Plato's *Republic*. The story is meant to illustrate how behaving immorally can sometimes be to one's advantage. If Gyges had remained virtuous, he would have remained poor. By breaking the moral rules, however, he became rich and powerful. Considering this, why should Gyges care about the moral rules? For that matter, why should any of us be moral if it doesn't serve our own needs? Why tell the truth, if lying is more convenient? Why give money to charity, when you can spend it on yourself? Morality places restrictions on us that we may not like. So why shouldn't we just forget about it? Glaucon adds that, in his opinion, all of us would behave like Gyges, if we thought we could get away with it.

In what follows, we will take up the question of why we should be moral. But first, we need to understand the question. It is not a request for a justification of moral behavior. If it were,

153

then the answer would be easy. We could easily say why Gyges shouldn't have robbed and murdered his way to the throne. Robbery is taking things that do not belong to you, and murder inflicts a terrible harm on its victims. Similarly, it is easy to explain why we should be truthful or why we should give money to help the needy. Lying harms people, and hungry people need food more than people like us need money.

Such reasons, however, only determine what is right, and that is not the issue. Glaucon's challenge arises after the moral reasoning has been done. We may grant that it is morally right to respect people's lives and property. We may concede that it is right to tell the truth and help people. Glaucon's question is, *Why should we care about doing what is right?*

To answer this question, we must show that living morally is in our own best interests, and that will not be easy. On the surface, it looks like ethics is a hindrance in promoting one's own happiness. Of course, it may be a good thing for you if *other people* live ethically, for then they will respect your rights and be helpful to you. But if *you* are bound by moral constraints, that is another matter.

Can it be shown that accepting moral constraints really is in one's self-interest? We might be able to meet Glaucon's challenge, and we might not. It all depends on what morality is.

12.2. Ethics and Religion

One familiar idea is that right living consists in obedience to God's commands. On this conception, God has set out the rules we must obey, and he will reward those who follow his rules and punish those who do not.

If this were true, we could answer Glaucon's challenge as follows: We should be moral because otherwise God will punish us. Even if, like Gyges, we had the power of invisibility, we would still be visible to God, and so, ultimately, we could not get away with being wicked. In one familiar scenario, the righteous will spend eternity in heaven while the sinners will go to hell. Thus, any benefit you might gain from wrongdoing will be only temporary. In the long run, virtue pays.

That response, however, may not fully answer Glaucon's challenge. On the familiar scenario, God does not reward individuals in proportion to their virtue. Rather, God sorts everyone into just two groups: the heaven-bound and the hell-bound. In the end, both the saints and those who barely scrape by wind up in the same heavenly paradise. Thus, it might be to your advantage to do just enough to get into heaven, but no more. And so, you can ask: Why should I be moral, when a little immorality will benefit me on earth without spoiling my chances at heaven?

On these assumptions, Glaucon's challenge can be partly answered: Even if we can get away with some immorality, we shouldn't risk hellfire by robbing and murdering our way to the throne. But in fact, much more virtue than that might be called for. In examining our own lives, we can never be too sure as to what God might be thinking. You never know when one more selfish act might tip the scales. Thus, we should probably be as good as we can be, to increase our chances of eternal bliss.

Let's now discuss, more generally, the moral theory that puts God in the center of things. According to the Divine Command Theory, an action is morally right if, and only if, it is commanded by God. Is this theory correct? If we tried to live by it, we would encounter enormous practical difficulties. How can we know what God commands? Some people claim that God has told them what he wants us to do. But why should we trust those people? Hearing voices can be a sign of schizophrenia, and anyway, they might be lying. They might be saying they've spoken to God merely to get attention, or to feel important, or to persuade their followers to send them money.

Others rely, more modestly, on Scripture and Church tradition for guidance. But those sources are notoriously difficult to interpret. They give vague and sometimes contradictory instructions. So, when people consult these authorities, they typically rely on their own judgment to sort out what seems acceptable. For example, they may cite the passage in Leviticus that condemns homosexuality while ignoring the passage that requires you to wash your clothes if you touch anything a menstruating woman has sat upon.

But these are just practical difficulties. It may still seem plausible that God's commands provide the ultimate basis for ethics: God's saying that something is wrong is what *makes it* wrong. Many religious people think it would be sacrilege not to accept this view. Socrates, however, gave a powerful argument against it.

In the *Euthyphro,* Socrates considers whether "right" can be the same as "what the gods command." Socrates accepted that the gods exist and that they may issue instructions. But he showed that this cannot be the ultimate basis of ethics. As he said, we need to distinguish two possibilities: Either the gods have good reasons for their instructions, or they do not. If they do not, then their commands would be arbitrary—the gods would be like petty tyrants who demand that we do this and that even though there is no good reason for it. This is an impious view that religious people will not want to accept. On the other hand, if the gods do have good reasons for their instructions, then there must be a standard of rightness independent of their commands—namely, the standard which they themselves adhere to in deciding what to require of us.

It follows, then, that the rightness or wrongness of actions cannot be understood merely in terms of their conformity to divine commands. We may always ask why the gods command what they do, and the answer to that question will reveal why right actions are right and why wrong actions are wrong.

The same is true of sacred texts. Nothing can be morally right or wrong simply because a book says so. If the book's decrees are not arbitrary, then there must be some reason for them. For example, the Bible says we should not lie about our neighbors—we should not "bear false witness" against them. Is this rule arbitrary? Certainly not. Lying causes harm and violates the trust that others have in us, and lying about our neighbors is insulting to them. *That's* why lying is wrong. The reason is not, "because the Bible says so." Similarly, we may ask why homosexuality is condemned. Are there good reasons for this pronouncement? If so, then those reasons will give the real explanation of why homosexuality is wrong. If not, then homosexuality isn't wrong, and the Bible's condemnation is unjustified.

These problems make the Divine Command Theory implausible, but they do not refute the separate idea that, if God punishes wrongdoing, then we have good reason to be moral. This idea so impressed the great German philosopher Immanuel Kant (1724–1804) that he made it into an argument for God's existence. Kant reasoned that if God does not exist, then the universe is morally incomplete, because virtue will go unrewarded and wickedness will go unpunished. This thought was intolerable to him, so he concluded that God exists. Even great philosophers, it seems, can indulge in wishful thinking.

12.3. The Social Contract

In the seventeenth century, with the rise of modern science, philosophy became an increasingly secular enterprise. Since then, there has been a rough consensus that ethics must be understood as a human phenomenon—as the product of human needs, interests, and desires.

Thomas Hobbes (1588–1679) was the first great modern thinker to offer a secular basis for ethics. Hobbes assumed that "good" and "bad" are what we call the things that we like or dislike. Thus, when you and I like different things, we regard different things as good or bad. However, Hobbes said, we are all essentially alike. We are all self-interested creatures who want to live as well as possible. This is the key to understanding ethics. Ethics arises when people realize what they must do to live as well as they can.

Hobbes points out that each of us is enormously better off living in a cooperative society than trying to make it on our own. The benefits of social living go far beyond companionship. Social living makes possible schools, hospitals, and highways; houses with electricity and central heating; airplanes and cell phones; books, magazines, and websites; movies, opera, and football; and science, engineering, and agriculture. Without social cooperation, we would lose all of this. Therefore, it benefits each of us to establish and maintain a cooperative society.

But it turns out that a cooperative society can exist only if we adopt certain rules of behavior—rules that require telling the truth, keeping our promises, respecting one another's lives and property, and so on:

- If people couldn't be relied on to tell the truth, then no one would care what anyone said. Communication would be impossible. And without communication, society would collapse.
- If people didn't keep their promises, then there could be no division of labor—workers could not count on getting paid, retailers could not rely on their suppliers, and so on—and the economy would collapse. There could be no business, no building, no agriculture, and no medicine.

- Without assurances against assault, murder, and theft, no one could feel secure. Everyone would have to be constantly on guard, and no one could trust their neighbors.

Thus, to obtain the benefits of social living, we must strike a bargain with one another, whereby each of us agrees to obey these rules. This "social contract" is the basis of morality. Thus, morality may be understood as *the rules that a self-interested person would agree to obey, provided that others agree to obey them as well.*

Why the Social Contract Theory Is Attractive. This way of thinking about morality has a number of appealing features. First, it takes the mystery out of ethics and makes it a practical, down-to-earth business. Living morally is not a matter of blind obedience to the mysterious dictates of a supernatural being. Instead, it is about doing what it takes to make social living possible.

Second, the social contract approach gives us a sensible way of determining what our moral duties are. We are morally required to do the things that make social living possible. Otherwise, we may do what we like. Unfortunately, when many people hear the word "morals," they think about an attempt to restrict their sex lives. But an ethic based on the social contract would have little interest in people's personal affairs.

Third, the Social Contract Theory gives a plausible answer to Glaucon's question: Why should we behave morally when it is not to our advantage? Well, it *is* to our advantage to live in a society in which people behave morally. Thus, it is rational for us to accept moral restrictions on our conduct, because the overall system benefits us. There is, however, a problem with this answer.

The Problem of the Free Rider. Schemes of social cooperation always face the "free rider" problem. A free rider is someone who benefits from a cooperative arrangement without contributing to it. Suppose the home owners in my neighborhood chip in to pay for a streetlight. I want the light as much as anyone else does, but I refuse to chip in, knowing that they will go ahead without me. The light is installed, and I get to use it for free. That makes me a free rider.

In any cooperative society, there will be some free riders—individuals who benefit from living in the society, but who don't follow the rules which make the society possible. Glaucon's challenge may therefore be reformulated: Why not be a free rider? Each of us already enjoys the benefits of living in a stable society. So, why shouldn't we break the rules if we think we can get away with it?

The free-rider problem for ethics can be solved, but only partially. The partial solution goes like this: Each of us has good reason not only to encourage others to obey the social rules but also to make it as hard as possible for them to break those rules. Take the rule against murder, for example. You don't merely want to encourage others not to murder you. You want a situation in which *no one can get away with* murdering you. Each of us has good reason to support the creation and maintenance of a social system in which other people could not murder us. To accomplish this, we establish laws and other methods of enforcement. But in doing so, we create a situation in which *we* cannot get away with murder, either.

I said that this is a "partial" solution, for two reasons. First, we use the power of the law to enforce the rules against murder, theft, and other grave offenses, but not all social rules are suitable for legal enforcement. Rules of ordinary decency must be enforced in "the court of public opinion" rather than in the court of law. The penalty for lying, for example, is only that people will get angry at you. Although everyone wants to avoid prison, not everyone minds upsetting the people around them. Thus, informal methods of enforcement are bound to be only partly effective.

Second, no mechanisms, formal or informal, are going to be perfect. It is easy to get away with the occasional lie. One might even get away with the occasional murder. Glaucon's challenge remains: Why should you obey the moral rules when you think you can get away with breaking them?

12.4. Morality and Benevolence

The Social Contract Theory does not assume that people are altruistic. Each person can be motivated to obey the social rules out of simple self-interest. However, people are not entirely selfish. Human beings have at least some benevolent feelings, if only for family and friends. We have evolved as social creatures just as surely as we have evolved as creatures with lungs. Caring for our kin and members of our local group is as natural for us as breathing.

If humans do have some degree of natural altruism, does this have any significance for ethics? David Hume (1711–1776), the great Scottish philosopher, thought so. Hume agreed with Hobbes that our moral opinions are expressions of our feelings, but he did not believe that our feelings are merely self-centered. He believed that we also have "social sentiments"—feelings that connect us with other people and make us care about them. That is why, Hume says, we measure right and wrong by "the true interests of mankind":

> In all determinations of morality, this circumstance of public utility is ever principally in view; and wherever disputes arise, either in philosophy or common life, concerning the bounds of duty, the question cannot . . . be decided with greater certainty than by ascertaining . . . the true interests of mankind.

This view came to be known as Utilitarianism. In modern moral philosophy, it is the chief alternative to the Social Contract Theory.

Utilitarianism. Utilitarians believe that one principle sums up all our moral duties: *We should always try to produce the greatest possible benefit for everyone who will be affected by our action.*

This Principle of Utility is deceptively simple. It actually combines three ideas. First, in determining what to do, we should be guided by the consequences of our actions—we should do whatever can be reasonably expected to have the best outcome. Second, in determining which consequences are best, we should care only about the benefits and harms that would be caused—we should do whatever will cause the greatest benefits and the least significant harms. And third, the Principle of Utility assumes that each person's happiness is as important as anyone else's.

Although Hume suggested this idea, two philosophers from England pursued it in greater detail. Jeremy Bentham (1748–1832) led a movement to reform the laws of Britain along utilitarian lines. The Benthamites were remarkably successful in advancing such causes as prison reform and restrictions on the use of child labor. John Stuart Mill (1806–1873), the son of a Benthamite, gave the theory its most popular and influential defense in his book *Utilitarianism.*

The utilitarian movement attracted critics from the outset. It was an easy target because it ignores conventional religious notions. Morality, according to the Utilitarians, has nothing to do with obedience to God or gaining credit in heaven. Rather, the point is just to make life in this world as comfortable and as happy as possible. Thus, some critics condemned Utilitarianism as a godless doctrine. To this Mill replied:

> [T]he question depends upon what idea we have formed of the moral character of the Deity. If it be a true belief that God desires, above all things, the happiness of his creatures, and that this was his purpose in their creation, utility is not only not a godless doctrine, but more profoundly religious than any other.

Utilitarianism was also an easy target because it rejected many conventional moral notions. Bentham argued, for example, that the purpose of the criminal justice system cannot be understood in the traditional way as "paying back" offenders for their wicked deeds—that only piles misery upon misery. Instead, the social response to crime should be threefold: to identify and deal with the causes of criminal behavior; where possible, to reform individual lawbreakers and make them into productive citizens; and to "punish" people only insofar as it is necessary to deter others from committing similar crimes. Today these ideas are familiar, but only because the utilitarian movement was so successful. Or, to take a different example: By insisting that everyone's happiness is equally important, the Utilitarians offended various elitist notions of group superiority. According to the utilitarian standard, neither race nor sex nor social class makes a difference to one's moral status. Mill himself wrote a book called *The Subjection of Women* that became a classic of the nineteenth-century suffragist movement.

Finally, Utilitarianism was controversial because it has no use for "absolute" moral rules. According to Utilitarianism, the traditional moral rules are merely "rules of thumb"—they're good pieces of advice, but they admit of exceptions. Whenever breaking a rule will have better results than following the rule, we should break it. The rule against killing, for example, might be suspended if someone is dying of a painful illness and requests a painless death. Moreover, the Utilitarians regard some traditional rules as suspect, even as rules of thumb. Christian moralists had traditionally said that masturbation is evil, but from a utilitarian point of view, masturbation is a good thing. A more serious matter is the religious condemnation of homosexuality, which has resulted in misery for countless people. Utilitarianism implies that if an activity makes people happy, without anyone being harmed, it cannot be wrong.

Utilitarianism says that our moral duty is to promote the general happiness. Why should we do that? Mill echoes Glaucon's challenge when he says, "I feel that I am bound not to rob or murder, betray or deceive; but why am I bound to promote the general happiness? If my own happiness lies in something else, why may I not give that the preference?" Aside from the "external sanctions" of law and public opinion, Mill saw only one possible reason for accepting this or any other moral standard. The "internal sanction" of morality, he said, must always be "a feeling in our minds." And the kind of ethic we accept, he thought, will depend on the nature of our feelings. If human beings have "social feelings," then Utilitarianism will be the natural standard for them:

> The firm foundation [of utilitarian morality] is that of the social feelings of mankind—the desire to be in unity with our fellow creatures, which is already a powerful principle in human nature, and happily one of those which tend to become stronger, even without express inculcation, from the influences of advancing civilization.

Impartiality. Utilitarianism has implications that conflict with traditional morality. Much the same could be said about the Social Contract Theory. In most of the practical matters that we have mentioned—criminal punishment, racial discrimination, women's rights, euthanasia, homosexuality—the two theories agree. But they differ dramatically on one issue. Utilitarians, but not social contract theorists, think that we have an extensive moral duty to help others.

Suppose, for example, you are thinking of spending $1,000 for a new living room carpet. Should you do this? What are the alternatives? One alternative is to give the money to an agency such as the United Nations Children's Fund (UNICEF). Around 8.8 million children under the age of 5 die each year, mostly from preventable causes such as pneumonia, diarrhea, malaria, and birth asphyxia. By giving your money to UNICEF and making do with your old carpet, you could provide life-saving medical care for dozens of children. From the point of view of utility—seeking the best overall outcome for everyone—there is no doubt that you should give the money to UNICEF. Obviously, the medicine will help the children far more than the new rug will help you.

The Social Contract Theory takes a different approach. If morality rests on an agreement between people—an agreement we enter into to promote our own interests—what would the agreement say about helping other people? It depends on whether those other people can help us. If they can, then we could benefit from an agreement to help each other. If not, then we have no reason to accept any restrictions on our conduct.

From this point of view, we would have no reason to accept a general duty to provide aid to children in foreign countries. Jan Narveson, a social contract theorist, says that we needn't "go very far out of our way to be very helpful to those we don't know and may not particularly care for." And, Narveson asks,

> What about parting with the means for making your sweet little daughter's birthday party a memorable one, in order to keep a dozen strangers alive on the other side of the world? Is this something you are morally required to do? Indeed not. She may well *matter* to you more than they. This illustrates again the fact that people do *not* "count equally" for most of us. Normal people care more about some people than others, and build their very lives around those carings.

Which view is correct? Do we have a moral duty to help strangers or not? Here is a thought experiment that might help. Suppose there are two buttons on my desk, and I must choose which to press. By pressing button A, I can provide my daughter with a memorable party; by pressing button B, I can save the lives of a dozen strangers. Is it really all right for me to press A just because I care more for my daughter? What would your "conscientious feelings" tell you? Mill believed that one's conscientious feelings—the feelings that prevail after everything has been thought through—determine one's obligations. He believed that we cannot, when we are thoughtful and reflective, approve of pushing button A.

However, some contemporary Utilitarians have argued that the matter need not be left to the uncertainties of individual feeling. Their argument goes like this: It may be true that we all care more for ourselves, our family, and our friends than we care for strangers. But we have rational capacities as well as feelings, and if we use those, we will realize that there are no relevant differences between us, those close to us, and strangers. Strangers have needs and interests, just like we do. Thus, no one should take his or her own well-being to be especially important. Peter Singer (1946–), a utilitarian philosopher, writes:

> Reason makes it possible for us to see ourselves in this way. . . . I am able to see that I am just one being among others, with interests and desires like others. I have a personal perspective on the world, from which my interests are at the front and centre of the stage, the interests of my family and friends are close behind, and the interests of strangers are pushed to the back and sides. But reason enables me to see that others have similarly subjective perspectives, and that from "the point of view of the universe," my perspective is no more privileged than theirs. Thus my ability to reason shows me the possibility of detaching myself from my own perspective, and shows me what the universe might look like if I had no personal perspective.

So, from an objective viewpoint, each of us must acknowledge that our own perspective—our own particular set of needs, interests, likes, and dislikes—is only one among many and has no special status. Morally, everyone counts equally, even strangers in foreign countries who have no ability to help us or harm us.

Conclusion. We have reached no firm conclusions about what morality requires of us. However, it looks like morality requires us to care about the needs and interests of total strangers. But why should we do that? Glaucon's challenge remains: Why should we do what's right, if there's nothing in it for us?

A religious outlook that includes a belief in the afterlife could help us answer Glaucon's question. Otherwise, we can appeal to the fact that everyone benefits from a social arrangement in which the moral rules are acknowledged and enforced. But the free-rider problem cannot be completely solved; people can always get away with a certain amount of bad behavior. In the end, we can only hope that people's behavior will be guided by what Mill called "the conscientious feelings of mankind."

This may seem like a feeble conclusion. Yet "the conscientious feelings of mankind" are a powerful force, made stronger by education and the advancement of civilization. Still, we must concede that, if people can get away with wrongdoing and genuinely don't care about others, then nothing will stop them. We could remind them of all the reasons why their actions would be wrong and remind them that their interests don't matter more than the interests of other people. But that will only prove that their actions *are* wrong. To stop them from behaving badly, something more is required, namely, that they care about those reasons.

CHAPTER 13

The Meaning of Life

Death's at the bottom of everything.
—Graham Greene, *The Third Man* (1950)

13.1. The Problem of the Point of View

In 1826 John Stuart Mill became obsessed with the thought that his life was meaningless. He was only 22 years old, and his great works were still ahead of him, but he had already begun to make a name for himself. He wrote for a radical journal founded by Jeremy Bentham, the great utilitarian philosopher, and he often spoke on behalf of progressive causes. "I had what might truly be called an object in life," Mill said, "to be a reformer of the world." But then he suddenly lost confidence. His work no longer seemed important to him. He came to believe that, even if he achieved everything he wanted, he would not be happy. "I was in a dull state of nerves," Mill said, "… I seemed to have nothing left to live for." This condition persisted for a year while outwardly he carried on as if nothing were wrong. But inwardly, the clouds grew darker.

Finally, as often happens in such cases, things turned around. Reading about a boy's reaction to his father's death, Mill was moved to tears, and he found his love of life returning:

> Relieved from my ever present sense of irremediable wretchedness, I gradually found that the ordinary incidents of life could again give me some pleasure; that I could again find enjoyment, not intense, but sufficient for cheerfulness, in sunshine and sky, in books, in conversation, in public affairs; and that there was, once more, excitement, though of a moderate kind, in exerting myself for my opinions, and for the public good. Thus the cloud gradually drew off, and I again enjoyed life.

One might understand Mill's experience as merely pathological: He was depressed, but eventually he snapped out of it. And that is probably true. But the meaning of life is a real problem that can arise even when we're not depressed. It is actually more than one problem, because different issues might be at stake. For Mill, the question was how to be happy. A different question is whether there is anything truly worth living for.

At the deepest level, the problem of the meaning of life arises from a clash between two points of view, each of which is natural and unavoidable for us. On the one hand, each of us occupies a personal point of view from which our lives and projects seem immensely important. We care about our family, our work, and whether the Red Sox will win the pennant. We have desires, goals, and plans. We are distressed by the fact that we will die, and on our deathbeds we regard that prospect as a calamity.

On the other hand, we can step outside our individual points of view and look at things from an impersonal standpoint. From "the point of view of the universe," our lives have little significance. What does it matter if I raise a family, succeed in my work, or take a trip to London? Eventually, I will die, and everything I do will come to nothing. In fact, the whole human race will vanish one day, leaving no trace behind.

The contrast could not be greater. From your own point of view, who you are and what you do are surpassingly important. But to the universe you are nothing. What are we to make of this? As Thomas Nagel (1937–) puts it, "In seeing ourselves from outside we find it difficult to take our lives seriously. This loss of conviction, and the attempt to regain it, is the problem of the meaning of life."

13.2. Happiness

The ancient philosophers had a lot to say about happiness. They assumed that human beings strive to be happy and that happiness consists in a life of reason and virtue. Epicurus (341–270 B.C.) recommended plain living, so as to avoid pains and anxieties. The Stoics added that a man should not let his happiness depend on things he can't control, like wealth, health, good looks, and the opinion of others. We cannot control external events, they said, so we should be indifferent to them and take life as it comes. Epictetus (ca. A.D. 55–135), one of the great Stoic teachers, told his students, "Ask not that events should happen as you will, but let your will be that events should happen as they do."

In recent years, happiness has been a hot topic in social science. In a typical "happiness study," the researcher will conduct a large survey, asking people how happy they are as well as their age, sex, race, religion, income level, educational history, political affiliation, and so on. Then the researcher will use statistical tools to look for significant results among the data. Using this method, investigators have discovered, for example, that the elderly tend to be happier than people in their 20s and 30s, and men tend to be happier than women.

Researchers have also discovered that happiness is largely genetic: Genes account for a whopping 80 percent of the variation in human happiness. That finding is confirmed by studies which show how *unimportant* environmental factors can be. Winning the lottery, for example, seems to have no long-term effect on happiness. People are ecstatic for a while, but in a few days the euphoria subsides: Grumpy people return to being grumpy, and cheerful people come down from the clouds but remain happy. The same is true of disasters. It took only three weeks for car crash victims in Michigan to become happy again, despite having suffered permanent, debilitating spinal cord injuries. Cancer patients also bounce back: They are unhappy upon learning their diagnosis, but soon they return to whatever level of happiness is normal for them.

Does wealth affect happiness? Everyone agrees that being impoverished is bad: People who lack necessities are less happy, on average, than those who have them. But suppose you have enough money to get by. Would having even more money make you happier? The answer seems to be, "Probably, but not as much as you might think."

Money, in general, is correlated with happiness in three ways: richer countries have happier citizens than poorer countries; as countries become richer over time, their citizens become happier; and, at any given moment, the richer people in a society tend to be happier than the poorer people. Together, these facts strongly suggest that income affects well-being. However, the impact is not very great. Remember, first, that genes account for about 80 percent of the variation in human happiness. Therefore, all the other factors, including wealth, can only account for about 20 percent. Second, recall that winning the lottery doesn't seem to provide any long-term boost in happiness.

If money made a huge difference to well-being, then presumably we could discern a difference in people's happiness before and after winning the lottery. Finally, these generalizations have exceptions. For example, Americans are four times richer than Mexicans, but Mexicans report being happier. Americans are three times richer than they were 50 years ago, but according to the surveys, they are no happier.

Happiness is also correlated with other things. One is personal control: People are happier being their own boss, for example, rather than taking orders from someone else. Another factor is good relations with others, especially friends and family. A third factor is meaningful work: People who feel that they are accomplishing something worthwhile report being especially happy. In general, happiness is self-sustaining, because happy people tend to behave in ways that keep them happy. They have higher opinions of other people and are more outgoing. Thus, they form friendships more easily. Happy people are also more optimistic. They tend to choose long-term rewards over short-term satisfactions.

You might think, then, that in order to be happier you need to take control of your life, make friends, and seek out meaningful work. All that may be true, but there is a catch. If you value these things only as a means to your happiness, then they will not make you happy. Happiness cannot be sought directly. Instead, you must value friends and work in their own right. Happiness is then the welcome by-product. As John Stuart Mill said, "Ask yourself if you are happy, and you cease to be so. The only chance is to treat, not happiness, but some end external to it, as the purpose of life."

13.3. Death

Some people believe that even a happy life can be meaningless. After all, they say, we will inevitably die, and anyway, the universe doesn't care about us. We'll consider these ideas in turn.

What attitude should we take toward our mortality? It depends, of course, on what we believe happens when we die. Some people believe they will live forever in paradise. Death, therefore, is like moving to a much better neighborhood. If you believe this, you should think that death is a wonderful thing, for you will be much better off after you die. Apparently, Socrates had this attitude, but most people do not.

On the other hand, death may be the permanent end of your existence. When you die, you're gone. It is important to understand what this means. Some people assume that nonexistence is a hard-to-imagine condition. They ask, "What is it like to be dead?" and they expect a profound answer. But that is a mistake. We cannot imagine what it is like to be dead because there is nothing to imagine. What your life will be like in 2210 is what it was like in 1810.

If death is the end, what attitude should we take toward it? Most of us find it awful. We hate the thought of dying, and we are willing to do almost anything to prolong our lives. Epicurus, however, said that we should not fear death. In a letter to one of his followers, he argued that "Death is nothing to us," because when we are dead we do not exist, and if we do not exist nothing can harm us. We will not be unhappy; we will suffer no pain; we will not be afraid, worried, or bored; and we will have no regrets. Therefore, Epicurus concluded, the wise person will not fear death.

There is something to this. However, it overlooks the fact that death is bad because it is a huge deprivation—if our lives could continue, we could enjoy all sorts of things. Thus, death is an evil because it puts an end to the good things of life. After I die, human history will continue, but I won't get to be a part of it. I will see no more movies, read no more books, make no more friends, and take no more trips. If my wife survives me, I will not get to be with her. I will not know my grandchildren's children. New inventions will appear and new discoveries will be made about the nature of the universe, but I won't know what they are. New music will be composed, but I won't hear it. Perhaps we will make contact with intelligent beings from other planets, but I won't know about it. That is why I don't want to die, and Epicurus's argument is beside the point.

But does the fact that I am going to die make my life meaningless? After all, it is said, what is the point of working, making friends, and raising a family if, in the end, we will all turn to dust? This thought has a certain emotional resonance, but it involves a fundamental mistake. We must distinguish the value of a thing from how long that thing will last. Something can be good while it lasts, even though it will not last forever. For example, in Afghanistan the Taliban destroyed a number of ancient monuments of great beauty and religious significance. Yet we would never say that these monuments lacked value, just because their time on earth was limited. A human life can also be wonderful, even though it must end.

At the very least, the mere fact that it will end does not extinguish whatever value it has.

13.4. Religion and the Indifferent Universe

From the point of view of the universe, it is said, human life has no significance. W. B. Yeats (1865–1939), the great Irish poet, put this matter in chilling perspective:

> Where are now the warring kings,
> Word be-mockers?—By the Rood,
> Where are now the warring kings?
> An idle word is now their glory,
> By the stammering schoolboy said,
> Reading some entangled story:
> The kings of the old time are dead;
> The wandering earth herself may be
> Only a sudden flaming word,
> In clanging space a moment heard,
> Troubling the endless reverie.

Warring kings must die, the wandering earth is an insignificant speck, and the whole history of the human race is only a blip in time. In light of this, how can we attach any meaning to what we do?

One way to overcome this problem is to adopt a religious point of view according to which the universe is *not* indifferent to us. The great monotheistic religions—including Judaism, Christianity, and Islam—believe that God created the universe to provide a home for us and that our destiny is to live with Him forever. Human life is not, therefore, a meaningless blip in the history of the universe. Instead, we are the leading stars in the whole cosmic drama.

I will leave aside the question of whether the religious story is true, in order to ask a different question. Suppose it is true. How does the religious story help us understand the meaning of life? This question turns out to be puzzling.

Perhaps our lives are meaningful because *God has a plan for us.* But it is hard to see how the intentions of an outside agent could make your life meaningful to you. Suppose your parents have a plan for you: They want you to become a doctor. You might find this agreeable; but you might find it smothering, because you want to make your own plan. Indeed, if an outside force dictates the terms of your life, you might regard your life as having no meaning at all.

Another possibility is that our lives are meaningful because *we are the objects of God's love.* According to the great religions, the universe isn't indifferent to us; rather, its Creator and Overseer cares about us deeply. But again, though this might be comforting, it is hard to see how it helps. If love is needed to give our lives meaning, most of us already have that. We have family and friends who care about us, and we care about them. If we think that our lives lack meaning despite this, how is the addition of someone else's love supposed to help?

Finally, from a religious point of view, human life is seen as a *permanent* feature of the universe. Death is overcome. But we have already considered this thought. The duration of a life is separate from its meaning. Indeed, an eternal life might be meaningless if it is devoid of everything that makes life worthwhile. And a short life might be full of worthwhile things.

Religion *can* help us understand the meaning of life, but so far we haven't considered a key element of religious belief. That element is the believer's own commitment. She willingly accepts her role as God's child and chooses to adopt a way of life that goes with it. This is important, because when she embraces her religion, it is no longer being imposed on her from the outside. Instead, those values become her own. She lives a religious life "from the inside," as a matter of conviction. Her life then gets its meaning from the things that she values: God's plan for her, God's love, and her own involvement in the religious life of her community.

But note that her life has meaning, not because she pursues *religious* values, but because she pursues *her own values.* And she might value something else. For example, she might see herself as a scholar, an athlete, a chess player, a musician, or a businessperson. Like Mill, she might strive "to be a reformer of the world." Then her life would get its meaning from the values associated with those activities, just as her life now gets its meaning from her religion.

Religion does have one great advantage over these other ways of finding meaning: It solves the problem of the indifferent universe. If, like Mill, you take it as your goal to reform the world, you must still face the fact that the universe doesn't care. That is why it is so tempting to say that, without God, life is meaningless. At the same time, however, the religious commitment has a drawback that the other commitments do not have: It assumes that the religious story is true. We do not want to base our lives on moonshine; if the religious story is not true, we are doing just that.

13.5. The Meaning of Particular Lives

There is a difference between *life's* having a meaning and *a life's* having a meaning. If the religious story is true, then human life in general has a meaning. Without religion, we can only say that each life has its own particular meaning and that what our lives mean is up to us.

The comedian Groucho Marx once said, "Those are my principles. If you don't like them, I have others." Hopefully, your own principles mean more to you than Groucho's meant to him. Embracing your values will always add meaning to your life, if you are truly embracing them. *What* you value will depend on your talents, dispositions, and beliefs. Think of Socrates, St. Francis, Yogi Berra, Jonas Salk, Marilyn Monroe, Mohandas Gandhi, Ruth Graham, Bill Gates, Agatha Christie, Nelson Mandela, Mick Jagger, your next-door neighbor, and your favorite professor. Clearly, there isn't one kind of life that all of these individuals should pursue. Different lives may be significant in different ways.

Despite this variety, however, it is easy to give a list of things that anyone might find meaningful:

- *Satisfying personal relationships.* Nothing in life contributes to individual happiness as much as loving people who love you back. That is why family and friends are so important.
- *Accomplishments one can be proud of.* You might take pride in what you achieve at school, at work, at home, in the gym, or in pursuit of your hobbies. If you're not proud of what you do, then it's hard to be happy, no matter how good your life is otherwise.
- *Aesthetic appreciation.* You can find beauty in many things, such as reading books, seeing *The Godfather,* playing over Bobby Fischer's chess games, listening to your favorite music, and watching a thunderstorm.
- *Enjoyable activities.* You might enjoy playing bridge, eating good food, shooting baskets, having sex, climbing mountains, traveling, quilting, or acting in a play.
- *Learning.* Learning satisfies one's curiosity and deepens one's understanding of the world. Ignorance is

rarely bliss; increasing one's knowledge is almost always satisfying.

- *Contributing to the welfare of others.* According to the studies, happy people are less self-absorbed than unhappy people and are more likely to help others in need. The studies also suggest that spending money on other people will make you happier than spending money on yourself. The ancients were right: Virtue does bring happiness.

There are many good things in life—so many, in fact, that it seems almost absurd for people to say that there's nothing worth living for.

Socrates's life was a combination of such things. He had a wife and children, and we are told that he was a faithful husband and father. His friends were devoted to him. He was a loyal Athenian who fought for his city in military campaigns. He enjoyed art and athletics. But above all, Socrates was dedicated to discovering the truth about the world. He lived in a time when not much was known, but his contribution to human understanding was immense. Through his teachings, Socrates opened up lines of thought that are still being explored today. And at the end of his life, he chose to die rather than betray the values he had lived for. It is easy to understand the meaning of his life—we need only reflect on all this.

However, it is also easy to be skeptical. In a certain frame of mind, people are attracted to the idea that really there is nothing to live for. They may concede that people *believe* various things to be worthwhile. But it is only an illusion. A hardheaded assessment, they say, exposes the truth: Life has no meaning.

Can the skeptic be answered? The only way to do so would be to consider the various things on our list, one at a time, and explain why each of them is meaningful. We can describe the ways in which personal relationships and accomplishments contribute to human happiness. We can expound on the glories of Mozart and the pleasures of basketball. We can observe that humans are by nature curious, and so we naturally want to understand the world. We can observe that human beings are social animals, so contributing to the welfare of others comes naturally to us.

Such reasoning may not show that our lives are "important to the universe," but it will accomplish something similar. It will show that we have good, objective reasons to live in some ways rather than others. When we step outside our personal perspectives and consider humanity from an impersonal standpoint, we still find that human beings are the kinds of creatures who can enjoy life best by devoting themselves to such things as family and friends, work, music, mountain climbing, and all the rest. It would be foolish, then, for creatures like us to live in any other way.